Interpretation

Concepts in the Study of Religion

Critical Primers

Series Editor:
K. Merinda Simmons, University of Alabama

Books in the series Concepts in the Study of Religion: Critical Primers offer brief introductions to an array of concepts—modes of analysis, tools, as well as analytic terms themselves—within the discourse of religious studies. Useful for almost any course, the volumes in the series do not attempt to assert normative understandings but rather they introduce and survey the various modes and contexts for scholarly engagement with the concept at hand. How, for example, has the term "myth" been used, and what can various definitions allow us to do as scholars? Who in the field is working on the category of race and how? What might be the future of scholarship on gender in religious studies? What are the possibilities and limitations of description or comparison as methodological approaches? Thus, these critical primers provide—but are not limited to—concise overviews of the history of an approach or term. They also present the authors' own critical analyses of the dynamics and stakes present in discourses surrounding these concepts. Including lists of further readings to guide additional consideration of their topic, the books in this series are valuable resources for students and advanced scholars alike.

The series is published in association with the North American Society for the Study of Religion (NAASR).

Published

Comparison
Aaron W. Hughes

Interpretation

A Critical Primer

Nathan Eric Dickman

SHEFFIELD UK   BRISTOL CT

Published by Equinox Publishing Ltd.

UK: Office 415, The Workstation, 15 Paternoster Row, Sheffield, South Yorkshire S1 2BX

USA: ISD, 70 Enterprise Drive, Bristol, CT 06010

www.equinoxpub.com

First published 2023

© Nathan Eric Dickman 2023

All rights reserved. No part of this publication may be reproduced or transmitted in any form or by any means, electronic or mechanical, including photocopying, recording or any information storage or retrieval system, without prior permission in writing from the publishers.

British Library Cataloguing-in-Publication Data
A catalogue record for this book is available from the British Library.

Library of Congress Cataloging-in-Publication Data

Names: Dickman, Nathan Eric, author.
Title: Interpretation : a critical primer / Nathan Eric Dickman.
Description: Sheffield, South Yorkshire ; Bristol, CT : Equinox Publishing Ltd, 2023. | Series: Concepts in the study of religion | Includes bibliographical references and index. | Summary: "This volume examines the nature of interpretation, strategies within interpretation, and negotiations about the adequacy of an interpretation, with special attention paid to possible roles interpretation plays in the academic study of religions. Each chapter of this book refines a conceptual element that combines with others into a theory of interpretation useful for the classroom and in scholarship on hermeneutics"—Provided by publisher.
Identifiers: LCCN 2023009542 (print) | LCCN 2023009543 (ebook) | ISBN 9781800503366 (hardback) | ISBN 9781800503373 (paperback) | ISBN 9781800503380 (pdf) | ISBN 9781800504042 (epub)
Subjects: LCSH: Meaning (Philosophy) | Translating and interpreting.
Classification: LCC B105.M4 D53 2023 (print) | LCC B105.M4 (ebook) | DDC 121/.68—dc23/eng/20230602
LC record available at https://lccn.loc.gov/2023009542
LC ebook record available at https://lccn.loc.gov/2023009543

ISBN-13 978 1 80050 336 6 (hardback)
         978 1 80050 337 3 (paperback)
         978 1 80050 338 0 (ePDF)
         978 1 80050 404 2 (ePub)

Typeset by JS Typesetting Ltd, Porthcawl, Mid Glamorgan

Things are not all so comprehensible and expressible as one would mostly have us believe; most events are inexpressible, taking place in a realm which no word has ever entered ...
—Rainer Maria Rilke, *Letters to a Young Poet* (letter 1)

Contents

Acknowledgments	viii
Preface	ix
Introduction: What Is the Meaning of a Text?	1
1. The Predicaments of Interpretation	19
2. The Initiatives of Interpretation	42
3. The Medium of Interpretation	65
4. The Objects of Interpretation	91
5. The Practices of Interpretation	112
Conclusion: What Lies beyond Interpretation?	129
Appendix	136
Further Reading	137
References	139
Index	151

Acknowledgments

I am grateful for the invitation, encouragement, and support of Equinox's *Critical Primers* series editor, Merinda Simmons. I want to thank Merinda as well as two reviewers for their thoroughly constructive yet critical feedback—this has helped improve my text. I also want to thank current and former students, friends, and colleagues for their engagement with previous drafts—including Kandace McClure, Katherine Martinez Bojorquez. Maddy Windel, Gamyui Chan (Panchaneed Ratpiboon), Caley Smith, and Katherine Frank. This text builds upon and systematizes research and theorization in two of my other works, *Using Questions to Think* (Bloomsbury, 2021) and *Philosophical Hermeneutics and the Role of Questions in Religions* (Bloomsbury, 2022), as well as integrates multiple academic articles on related themes (see those listed in the reference list). However, the current text does not presuppose any previous engagement with these.

Preface

While I consider myself an expert in philosophy about interpretation, or philosophical hermeneutics, I do not consider myself a good interpreter. In fact, I often feel as if I am bad at interpreting. This is in part because I am not always clear what an interpretation even is. What distinguishes an interpretation from, say, an explanation? What differentiates translation and interpretation? Are interpretations just about your feelings toward whatever it is you are interpreting, or is there more to it? I also feel as if I am bad at interpretation because often when I try to interpret something, my efforts yield no fruit. When I try to read a manual explaining step by step how to assemble a bookshelf, I end up "winging it" instead of going through the document line by line, such as counting all the pieces or making sure which side of each board faces up or out. It is as if the manual is so boring that I directly get to assembling the shelves and only consult the manual once or if I run into issues. When I try to read financial documents or court documents, I often give up because I cannot grasp what they are saying. In these cases, it is as if the documents are in a foreign language and need to be translated. Often when I read poems or hear them recited, I find myself thinking it sounds pretty or find myself focused on a specific line that is especially pithy and clever. If someone were to ask me what the poem is about or what is being said about the topic, I would not be able to answer. When I read an argument—not in the sense of a fight or even a debate, but in the sense of a conclusion supported by premises—I do not feel I am interpreting, but merely following the inferential logic preserving truth of the premises in the conclusion. I am not interpreting, but merely understanding the claims and their support. I tend to avoid trying to interpret religious or sacred books because of how extreme and divisive groups get about their holy texts. It feels as if to them there is only one way to read or interpret their book, and it is socially risky to offer up an alternative perspective because they will react defensively, perhaps even violently. What will help us mitigate these contestations? My hope is that this book can serve as the kind of critically informed guide to "interpretation" that I need, and I suspect many of my readers can relate with me. While I explain my approach, argument, method, and book outline in the Introduction, I want to provide some preliminary remarks about the origins, purpose, and broader argumentative context of this project.

I have been fascinated by questions in the academic study of interpretation since I first enrolled in philosophy and religious studies courses. Yet even before that, in learning piano, percussion, and guitar during childhood, I already was fascinated by interpretation. How is it that my piano teacher could tell that my sister got a song just right, but that I always got it wrong even though I had the basic skills to play the song without any technical mistakes? Why is it called "reading" sheet music? How is it that some cover songs actually sound better than the original versions? These were some of the questions I found captivating. I just did not know these were questions connected to the study of interpretation until college.

My commitment to working on this project, to formulate a critical account of interpretation, solidified with regard to what many faculty members dread: "assessment." Many colleges and universities struggle with what to do for their core curriculum. Some colleges create categories aligned with institutional divisions, such as all students must take a couple Humanities courses, some courses in the Natural Sciences, some Social Science courses, and probably everyone has to take a writing, a speaking, and a math course. Other colleges have streamlined their core into solely the writing, speaking, and math courses. And still other colleges have created flexible categories that are not aligned with institutional divisions but are skill sets all graduating students should have, such as the ability to engage art, to quantify data, to analyze society, and to "interpret texts."

I once worked at a college that used this third model for the core curriculum. I was assigned to create an assessment plan for the "interpret texts" category, working with professors in Theater, Communication Studies, Literature, Art, History, Philosophy, Religious Studies, Environmental Studies, and more. That is, numerous courses were listed as options under the interpret texts category, courses specific to each of those programs. The assessment tool needed to be universal and standardized, showing how or whether students were learning to "interpret texts" through these listed Core courses. My proposal was flexible, appropriate for any reading assignment, asking two things:

(a) Can the student identify the main topic?

(b) Can the student indicate at least one thing being said about that main topic?

I believed these skills would be uncontroversial and would be assessed easily, creating a foundation for tracking student ability to interpret texts. However, what I thought would be an expedient and efficient discussion exploded into a philosophical debate about what constitutes a text and many objections to prioritizing reading written work. For example, some of the professors advocated that "dance" is a text. Still others advocated that "video games" are texts. You can probably tell already that this attempt to create a standardized assessment of student skills was abandoned. How could we create an assessment tool if we could not even reach consensus about what students were to interpret? Instead of a direct measure, I formulated an indirect measure that asked whether the students know that the course is supposed to help them learn to interpret texts better. This had the benefit of requiring professors to be explicit with themselves in their learning objectives and outcomes for a course, to be deliberate in ensuring the course explicitly states that it is about interpreting texts and that it actually helps students interpret texts better. An additional benefit is that now students themselves would be made more aware that this course on "religious scriptures" or "poetry" or "dance" or "video games" is in part for helping them interpret texts better. It was not a perfect solution, but it was a practical compromise.

Are dances and video games texts? Have you heard the phrase "read the room"? Are rooms things that can be read? Or consider "body language" and how sometimes people's actions speak louder than their words. I once heard an academic administrator give a speech to incoming freshman college students suggesting that they need to learn to read the "hidden curriculum." Can you read something that is hidden? Is there anything that is *not* a text? I raise these topics and questions not merely to highlight and complicate our assumptions about interpretation and reading. I also want to emphasize that there is good reason to be suspicious about overly prioritizing the written word. In criticism of white supremacist colonial patriarchy, we can identify many attributes, attitudes, and actions that help this system consolidate and maintain hegemonic power. For example, in the US, White people often respond defensively to questions or criticisms about their behaviors that have racist impact, a response that often deflects away from the impact of actions experienced by Black people and other persons of color to the deflector's inner and hidden intent (Olou 2019). For another example, there is a kind of paternalism among White people in the US where they feel entitled to make decisions on the part of others, as if White people know what is in others' best interests. As the antiracist activist Tema Okun explains, one attitude of white supremacism is what she labels "the worship of the written word" (Okun 2001). This involves devaluing other ways information is gathered and distributed, and also includes the perception of people with writing skills as more valuable to an organization and its mission. Are there alternative ways of documenting what is happening in a business meeting? Are emails and memos the only way to keep records or communicate?

My goal here is to emphasize how we need to be careful in developing a useful notion of interpretive practice. I want us to hold written texts as paradigmatic for interpretation, not dance or video games or other ways of preserving and sharing information. That is, I am choosing to prime us for and guide us through interpretation of written works. Ideally, this skill will prove transferable to other ways of expressing ourselves, such as dances and video games and hidden curriculums. However, in light of the above, if we use written texts as paradigmatic for interpretive practice, are we inadvertently complicit with maintaining white supremacy? Is my book itself an instance of worship of the written word? I want to formulate three responses to these questions and challenges to provide a defense of my project, hopefully in such a way that is not simultaneously defensive (and thus still explicitly complicit with white fragility).

First, I want to look more closely at what is problematic about *worshiping* the written word. I take this to indicate an inordinate imbuing of writing with nearly supernatural and mystical powers. White supremacist culture fetishizes written documents. Consider how the US Declaration of Independence, as an artifact or scroll with penned script on it, is treated not only in debates about what it means but especially in film and television. There are films focused on the acquisition of the "original" document (and its hidden messages) where barely a single instance of dialogue includes discussion of its expressed content. The implication is that if you have the written document, you have access to the power it holds, transmits, or represents. Hence Okun's point about emails and memos: it is the documents themselves, not necessarily their meanings or interpretations, that function as if they are amulets distributing power. This occurs in religious traditions as well. For example, in Nichiren Buddhist traditions, mere possession of and veneration of the *Lotus Sutra* is itself sufficient practice for transformation and the realization of nirvana. Or for a different example, consider the contemporary evangelical Christian fixation on the King James version of the Christian Bible, as if somehow this archaic English wording transmits the "Word of God" in ways that the original Greek or Hebrew does not. My point is that worship of the written word is more precisely the fetishization of the artifact. In the Introduction, I will forge a distinction between "book" and "text," but for now, the problematic kind of worship is of the book itself not the text expressed or interpreted via the book.

Second, by the time we get to the conclusion, I will restrict or reduce understanding solely to discourse—spoken, signed, or written complete thoughts. That is, other works in philosophical hermeneutics suggest interpretation is everywhere, that we can—at all times—interpret anything we want (Weiss 2008; Zigon 2018). The temptation is to treat all things as texts, such as mountains, star formations in the sky, weather, calendars, and people's inaction, anything (Parkes 2009; Foucault 2002). If we are always interpreting or if we are interpreting animals, then are not all things texts? The issue here is that this confuses two aspects of consciousness, taking features of the subjective pole of consciousness (noesis) as definitive for the objective pole of consciousness (noema)—as will be analyzed more thoroughly in Chapter 2. The fact that consciousness is primed to interpret, that our minds are structured to have limited perspectives and thus need to prioritize values and meanings, does not entail that all things have or express meanings. Not all objects are texts, and if we accept this, we are less likely to be disappointed when we do not understand some things. We inflate our understanding with the expectation and even the demand that all things we experience should be understood. We smear understanding across nearly all aspects of our lives, practically demanding that all things "should" be understandable even if in the end they are intrinsically *not* understandable. Unlike white supremacy that makes written books everything, in the superlative sense of that word, *my approach takes written works off the pedestal*, limiting our ability to interpret solely to texts. For anything else we might like to interpret, we are—by analogy—treating something that we know is not technically a text as if it is a text.

Third, intersecting traditions of thought about writing—specifically those that treat written prose as the pinnacle of free expression—influence my approach. For example, classical Chan (Zen) is notorious for promoting the transmission of the Dharma (or ultimate Truth) outside of words and letters. This is often taken to mean that the experience of "nirvana" transcends discursive or verbal thought. However, when we look closely at the preponderance of Zen literature circulating in Song Dynasty China (960–1279 CE), we can agree with many contemporary scholars of Chan that this critique is focused primarily on *empty* recitation of sutras (see Wright 2003, 264–265). Many Vajrayana or Tibetan Buddhists use prayer flags with mantras or sutras written on them, and when wind blows over them, the wind "recites" the mantras or sutras. In this way, the practitioners accumulate karmic merit. Likewise, many Song Buddhists constructed mechanical rotating bookshelves, moving the books as if they are being recited for karmic merit procurement (see Dickman 2022a, 162). This mode of "reading" puts books to use in ritual without attempting to interpret the texts. In this way, the Chan critique is ironic—pointing out that collectors do not understand the meanings of the books they claim to know. These readers fetishize the book itself rather than engaging the text in interpretation. For Chan masters, "genuine" reading and interpretation facilitates spiritual growth.

In early rabbinic Judaism, for another example, there is a narrative in the Talmud known as "The Hooks and the Crowns" (*Menachot 29B*). There, Moses—harassed by the Hebrews he liberated, who all want to return to Egypt—treks up Mt. Sinai to meet YHWH or *HaShem* to ask for help. He sees the Lord decorating letters of the Torah and is shocked by this since Moses needs help. The Lord says that one day a brilliant rabbi named Akiba will use all these decorative "hooks" and "crowns" to interpret scores and scores of *mitzvot* or Jewish regulations like kosher dietary rules. That is, the Lord seems to emphasize that writing or even calligraphy is more important than what appears to be urgent political needs for Moses.

In Islam, the medieval philosophical theologian and legal scholar Ibn Rushd argued that "poiesis" is higher than "mimesis" (see Gould 2014, 13). *Poiesis* is the Greek word from which the English word "poetry" is derived, but it has a broad application where through poetry or literary works we produce new worlds of meanings. *Mimesis* is the Greek word for imitation, both in the narrow sense of replicating, say, a bird's song, and in the broader sense of, say, theatrical performances where people act like other people. For Ibn Rushd, poiesis or verbal discourse allows for philosophy or freedom of thought, whereas imitation has too many constraints on it for sufficiently free philosophizing. Malcolm X expresses a similar sentiment when he states, "I have often reflected upon the new vistas that reading opened to me. I knew right there in prison that reading had changed forever the course of my life. As I see it today, the ability to read awoke inside me some long dormant craving to be mentally alive. I certainly wasn't seeking any degree, the way a college confers a status symbol upon its students" (X 1992, 206).

An additional intersecting influence on my approach is from early Continental philosophy in Georg Friedrich Wilhelm Hegel's work, specifically on the relations between forms of art and the freedom of thought. Hegel emphasizes that some forms of art, such as architecture and sculpture, are bound by determinations of space and time in such a way that these restrict our capacity for fully free expression and meaning (see Hegel 1997). He believes that music transcends limitations of space but not of time because music—principally defined by rhythm—maintains a connection to time. Poetry, however, is free from both space and time. Especially in the case of written works, we can share thoughts across vast distances of time or across different cultures. Yet, even poetry is limited because poetry—in his era (circa early 1800s)—was imagistic or representational (aka imitative). Thus it is really prose, conceptually clear or transparent discourse, that is genuinely free thinking.

I highlight these four intersecting influences on my approach not only because I take written works to be one kind of text among many other kinds of texts, like dance and video games. I also take discourse, especially writing, to be freer—or "higher" in Hegel's and Ibn Rushd's terms—than other media like that. However, this *does not mean* I am putting books on a pedestal. I will preserve a distinction between "books" and "texts," showing that it is impossible to put "texts" on a pedestal, even metaphorically, and that it is unhelpful to put books on a pedestal because then they will not get read.

I want to emphasize here that readers do not need to take my position about writing and thinking. What can be gained from my text is not based on taking a "side" about written works' superiority over other expressive forms and media. I share the above simply to lay my cards on the table in this Preface, and—perhaps—create a little intrigue for precocious readers who might disagree or agree or at least grasp the question to which the sides answer.

By the end of this text, I hope that we all feel more empowered to interpret for ourselves, and that, through expanding our horizons of understanding, we experience liberation from oppressive restraints that have prevented us from radical questioning and inhibited our capacity to grow.

University of the Ozarks
Clarksville, Arkansas
August 2022

Introduction

What Is the Meaning of a Text?

Sometimes interpretation seems instinctual, as if it is a straightforward ability we have once we learn how to speak, sign, and/or read. It often feels immediate, inasmuch as we do it seemingly without even thinking about it. Yet, as we will notice throughout this text, it is complex. Consider this imperative: "When you finish reading this sentence, rotate the book you're holding by 360°." Did you rotate the book just now? If you did not rotate the book, did you really understand the sentence? Or did you refuse to do it, even though you understood it? Did you feel embarrassed? Or is it that you did not explicitly refuse to follow along, but you are simply waiting for the main point of this illustration or for a more captivating hook for this Introduction to make sure reading this text is worth your time and effort? Did you know it was not a command but a mere illustration for what constitutes interpretation and understanding? The point I am trying to make with this illustration is that interpreting even a single sentence involves numerous factors and elements, from a reader's willingness to follow along to the broader context of a sentence within a book to even the broader social and economic context within which a book is written, printed, or read.

For the sake of introduction to my entire text, I want to argue for a few things to set the stage for our work together. I want to clarify how interpretation is everywhere, that it seems as if we are never not interpreting. Even people who claim they are not interpreting are—in fact—interpreting. I also want to distinguish between what I will call "texts" and "books" and explain how interpretation is something we do to texts and not to books. While your fellow readers might have their own physical book of this critical primer on interpretation, we all read the same text. To clarify understanding and interpretation, I further want to provide a scaffold from recognition of signs to understanding of sentences to interpretation of texts. This scaffold will serve as an antidote to our propensity to smear interpretation across distinct domains of our experience. I will conclude this chapter by providing a brief summary outline of my text, giving a preview of each chapter so we have a map of the terrain covered throughout the text.

Interpretation Is Ubiquitous

Interpreting seems to be ubiquitous, where we are always doing it in all our personal and social contexts. Consider debates you might have with friends about what a song means. What are Cardi B and Megan Thee Stallion saying in their hit, "W.A.P."? Are they critiquing the Women Against Pornography (WAP) movement of the 1980s (see Srinivasan 2021, 37)? Or consider all the popular interest in the interpretation of dreams. Or reflect on debates among legal scholars about the nature of the US Constitution. Is the correct reading of the law based on getting at the intentions of the founding figures or is the correct reading one that applies it within ever-evolving situations? One song popular during the winter holidays in the US is titled, "Baby it's cold outside." At one time it was seen as a sophisticated holiday hit, but now is perceived by many to be complicit with rape culture. When it comes to sacred traditions or books, we can see diverse interpretations represented in sects or denominations. For example, Nichiren Buddhists interpret the *Lotus Sutra* differently than Zen Buddhists. Or for another example, the Presbyterian Church (USA) interprets the Christian New Testament differently from the Presbyterian Church of America (PCA). That is, different people or groups of people get different things out of the same book. Or is it that different people and groups of people just project whatever their preferences are onto the same book? Is one side wrong and the other side right? Can there be a correct interpretation?

What is more, perhaps you yourself have had the experience where you reread the same book and got something different out of it the second time? Or maybe you listened to a song at one point in your life, but it took on a completely different significance at a later point in your life? Like the Four Tops' lyric goes: "It's the same old song, but with a different meaning since you've been gone." The same person can get different things out of the same book or song or film at different points in their life. Not only are interpretations everywhere, but these interpretations also often represent conflicts and competitions of interests between groups of people and their perspectives or conflicts and competitions of perspectives within a single person.

It is not just songs and books, right? Are we interpreting when our fingers pass across Braille? Are we interpreting when we see arrows or deer on street signs? How else would we know which way to turn or to slow down because an area is common for an animal crossing? Are we interpreting hoof prints in the snow on a hunt? Trackers use disturbances in brush and impressions in dirt and mud to detect a prey's path. Are we interpreting as soon as we wake up, such that—in a way—consciousness and interpretation are coextensive? Even to experience something *as* this or *as* that seems to involve an interpretive step from a chaotic mess of impressions to a semblance of organization of those impressions, like waking up disoriented and slowly realizing that you are waking up in a hotel on a vacation trip. Interpretation seems to involve this transition from one thing to another thing. For example, I have a coffee cup, but I use it as a penholder. Is that alternative use—from mug to penholder—an interpretation? Is it, rather, a *re*-interpretation? I raise these questions to complicate further the naivete we might have about interpretation.

Although Aristotle is often interpreted as defining human beings as "rational animals," that is a narrow translation of his Greek phrase ζῷον λόγον ἔχον (*zoon logon echon*) (Aristotle 2014, 428a20). Whereas *zoon* indicates animate life or the unique movement of a living thing, and *echon* denotes the principle or main thrust for a living thing's unique movement, at issue is how to approach the term *logon*. The *logon* is not just logic, but discourse and language in general, in such a way that it encompasses both reason and poetry. Human beings move through a sophisticated form of communication beyond gestures to articulate and expressive thought. As Aristotle states, "In this case of human beings what seems to count as living together is this sharing in dialogue and thought, not sharing the same pasture, as in the case of grazing animals" (Aristotle 1999, 1170b10–15). Unlike cows living alongside one another in physical proximity to one another, people require dialogue to bring them to a sense of closeness with one another. And this closeness can be achieved even if the people are not physically nearby one another, as often happens in forming new friendships through gaming or in maintaining longtime friendships over the phone or in creating classroom dialogue on Zoom during a pandemic. In other words, human beings live together through and by dialogue with one another. This dialogue, if written, can bridge historical distance as well, where we can feel connection with people who lived thousands of years ago through reading their written words.

More recent philosophers such as Charles Taylor redescribe human beings as "interpreting animals" (Taylor 1985). Because we have unique perspectives, we necessarily interpret our experiences and put our experiences into words, attempting to communicate our perspectives with others. That is, our differing perspectives and interpretations enable dialogue. Yet some people feel deflated or discouraged when others do not agree or do not "see eye to eye." Instead of experiencing disagreement or different perspectives as an opportunity for greater and more thorough dialogue, people experience these as threatening. Consider how defensive many religious fundamentalists get about even the slightest questioning of their dogmas. Perhaps this is an issue of disposition: are we "glass half full" or "glass half empty" types of people? Are differences opportunities for growth, or are they indications of our utter isolation and opposition to others? Our dialogues occur through our varying interpretations and perspectives.

However, many people do not conceive of their perspectives as interpretations. In fact, they perceive it as diminutive to call their perspective a "mere" interpretation. For them, all interpretation is biased and prejudiced. They do not interpret. Instead, they "amplify" what is there in the text. In religious contexts, many fundamentalists do not perceive themselves as biased in their reading of their scriptures, but that they use amplification to spread further what the text says. This happens in Christian circles, Buddhist circles, Muslim circles, and more. Some Wahhābist Muslims, for example, do not perceive themselves as interpreting the Quran or Hadiths but merely expressing what these are saying. The Hindutva movement in India often includes taking religious narratives literally, as if they are documenting past matters of facts, rather than interpreting poetic myths. That is, instead of seeing their religious traditions as interpretations of events, they take those traditions as transparent to the "facts themselves." Yet, as the sociologist of religions Reza Aslan elaborates,

> The fact is no evangelist in any of the world's religions would have been at all concerned with recording his or her objective observations of historical events. They would not have been recording observations at all! Rather, they were interpreting those events in order to give structure and meaning to ... their community, providing future generations with a common identity, a common aspiration, a common story. *After all, religion is ... interpretation.*
>
> (Aslan 2011, xxiv; my emphasis)

Moreover, this attempt to avoid appearing as an interpreter happens as much in literary circles as it does in religious contestations. As the literary critic Stanley Fish explains, many literary scholars disavow interpretation altogether and claim merely to describe classical works, to merely present classical books to readers for readers themselves to interpret the works for themselves (Fish 1980, 353). According to these religious practitioners and literary theorists, interpretation distorts the objective purity of texts whereas amplification conveys the objective meaning of texts. They would not say, "This is my interpretation." Instead, they say, "It says it right there in the text!" This strategy of claiming merely to amplify is itself a fantastic legitimation of a specific interpretation, but it is not really a way to avoid the fact that we seem never to not be interpreting. If I can hide from you that I am interpreting, then perhaps you will defer to my authority without questioning it!

It is especially naïve to claim merely to amplify texts. These practitioners and theorists neglect to rigorously distinguish between what usually is called *exegesis*, the grasping of a meaning expressed by a text, and *eisegesis*, the projecting into a text our own preferences for what we believe it should mean. Through exegesis, we attempt to listen to what a text has to say to us. Through eisegesis, however, we tell a book what it is saying. How do we make sure to get something out of reading a text rather than projecting whatever we prefer onto a book? How do we listen to rather than speak over others? Perhaps there is no perfect method to protect ourselves from making this mistake. We might be biased without even knowing it. The issue is whether we are open to revision or correction of what we—so far—take a text to be saying. Of course, we cannot avoid anticipating what a text might say. Our anticipation of possible meanings resembles sheer projection of our preferences, yet our anticipations are always subject to revisions through further engagement with a text.

Texts Are Not Books

A helpful way to address some of these problems is by forging compelling distinctions and designing our account of interpretation around those distinctions. A good distinction can open up a whole world for further exploration and research. As I mentioned in the Preface, we will be centering our account of interpretation around written works. Other artworks such as dances or video games might be considered texts, and my hope is that this critical primer will have much that can transfer to those types of work. My choice for written works will make more sense as we proceed further and further together in this account of interpretation, especially when we move into language and writing as they relate to our ability to interpret. For now, though, I want to note two things. First, written texts are explicitly linguistic phenomena and, as such, conveniently can be redescribed. It is always possible to put something said into other words or different words, especially—and perhaps essentially—"words" themselves. Second, note that by selecting written works as a paradigm for interpretation, this by no means implies a worship or fetishization of the written word. Such worship is complicit with a host of social and political ills, not least of which is white supremacy. We are saying neither that books somehow have more authority than dances, nor that books are more important than dances (even if some of my readers hold that prejudice). My goal is to develop a core of knowledge, skill, and disposition for interpretation that, ultimately, is transferable to other contexts for interpretation. Whatever we can do to written texts, we ought—ideally—to be able to do to other kinds of texts or other things that we treat *as* texts.

What is really worshipped is not texts, but books (or other documents), the material artifacts via which texts are transmitted. That is, a book is not a text, and a text is not a book, no matter how much the academic industry churns out the confused concept of a "textbook." Our distinction between "text" and "book" should open up a world for us to explore and examine. So, let us take our time to detail some differences between texts and books. If you were asked to distinguish between these two, how would you start? I mean, the words are literally different letters, right? But seriously, even if we generally treat the two words as synonyms, let us try to think of ways they are distinct. If they really were the exact same thing, would we need two words for it? Yet, even if they are different, they are definitely also related right? I suggest we isolate some differences between the words, such as the origins of the words, their different connotations, and more.

Where did the word "book" come from, and where did the word "text" come from? The word "book" comes from English transliteration from early Germanic references to beech trees and beech wood, where marks and letters were scratched into either the living trees themselves or into a tablet from the bark and wood. The French word for book, *livre*, derives from the Latin word for "the inner bark of trees," *librum*. Of course, the English word "library" came from here—the literal place where we store books and make them available to our community. Latin and Sanskrit cousins of the word "book" also have their basis in the names of trees, such as the birch tree or the ash tree. The word "book" used to refer to any written work but has come to refer primarily to a bound and fastened collection of many written pages or bound pages.

Consider some more uses for the word and its connotations. Why did the company that now refers to itself as "Meta" first use the name "Facebook"? Why not Facetext? The somewhat murky and likely skanky origins involved collecting women's faces with some information about them for a rolodex of potential dates. It bound faces into a book. What is contained in a telephone book or a cookbook? Telephone numbers, not telephones themselves, and recipes for cooking, not cooks themselves. Yet, do people ever call these "texts," as in a "cook-text"? Or consider the implication of calling someone "book-smart"? That suggests the person might know a lot of academic information, historical facts, and scientific findings. They keep their noses in books at the library. But they usually are somewhat clueless about the "streets," or the real world. Can we imagine calling someone "text-smart"? Gamblers place bets with "bookies," the people in charge of keeping records of bets, formerly in notebooks, and properly distributing the winnings and recuperating the losses. Why not call them "texties"? Sometimes groups of people gather together to make scrapbooks, not scraptexts. Or people book a flight or room, not text them. The phrase "one for the books" is a figure of speech to indicate an extraordinary event or personal achievement has taken place. Or consider when fascists burn or ban books. Is it possible to burn a text? The point of all of this is that the word "book" has very different origins and meanings from the word "text."

The English word "text" comes from Old French words for scriptures and treatises, such as *tixte*. And this French term derived from the earlier Latin word *textus*, which referenced the texture or style of a work, playing off of the meaning of *texere*, literally meaning to interweave, to fabricate, or to make wicker, such as with braided baskets. That is, the word "text" relates to the textile or clothing and fashion industry. What is written can be threaded together into a longer argument or story or account. Like fabric or cloth, a text weaves something together. But what exactly is it that is interwoven? Is it that the letters are like stitching or embroidery on the book page? We will return to this in more thorough detail in Chapter 4 on the objects of interpretation when we turn to look at how writing changes our experience and perception of discourse. For now, I want us to grasp that what is woven together is not ink or Braille on paper. We can see or feel or hear a sentence without understanding what it is saying or what it means. Instead, what is interwoven are thoughts, thoughts relevantly related to one another into a poem or argument or story or account or contract and so forth. Lines of thought or threads of thought are braided into bigger compositions, or in other words into texts. The book or bound paper tablets contain but are not equivalent to the text or fabric readers bring together through understanding what they are reading.

Consider some further uses and connotations of the word. We send text messages, not book messages, on our smartphones. While some people use emoticons or emojis, or other abbreviations and slang, most messages are brief. When someone writes in formal language or writes many sentences in a row in a single text message, they might be teased as sending a "book-length" message. To get a bit risqué, sometimes partners or new romantic interests will try to spice up their messages by "sexting," a combination of "sex" (or "sexy") and "texting." Would someone ever participate in "sooking" (combining "sexy" with "book")? The word also functions as the root for terms such as "context," "pretext," and "hypertext." A context is the meaningful situation or broader historical, material, and even personal matrix within which an event should be understood properly. Can we read Theravadin sutras out of context, or do we need to place them in their historical context to grasp what they mean? A pretext is how we dissimulate, how we express our reasons for what we are doing but in a way that misleads people. We pretend this is our reason, when we are using that to hide what we are really intending. A hypertext is more apparent in digital writing, where a word can be hyperlinked to another part of the website or a different website altogether. Consider entries in Wikipedia, for example, where numerous hyperlinks are included both for helpful navigation and for further and further research. Although this is most explicit with digital hyperlinks, it really is not a new phenomenon. Allusions, the poetic device of explicitly or implicitly referring to other parts of a work or other works, are themselves a kind of hyperlink in thought. In fact, we might best conceive of "context" as the name for the totality of relevant webs of hyperlinks related to a work.

I draw out these different connotations of the two words to indicate that most of us already have an intuitive grasp of their difference, and this difference will prove crucial in the account of interpretation I develop here. For now, I want to seal the fundamental difference between books and texts through the Jewish philosopher Martin Buber's clarification of two modes of relationality, what he calls the "I–It" mode of existence and the "I–Thou" mode of existence (Buber 1970). In the mode of the I–It, a subject stands above objects at its disposal. All these objects are mere things or tools to be used for the I's satisfaction and fulfillment. It is the essence of objectification, where everything is subordinate to it (see Nussbaum 1995). For Buber, this I does not "encounter" or enter into relationship with others, but solely experiences them. Like a tourist merely sightseeing, the I enjoys its experiences. Yet it lives in its world all alone. From this point forward, when I speak about "books," I am referring to this disposition toward the world, where we treat written works as material artifacts. Books are objects, mere things. These can be put on and taken off the shelf. Books can be burned. Texts, on the other hand, cannot be burned, but only understood and interpreted.

The other mode of existence, Buber's "I-Thou," involves intersubjectivity or genuine relationship with others. It is not just other persons, but also works of art, animals, nature, and even "spirits." For Buber, we do not experience others but rather *encounter* them. An encounter involves the realization that another person is not a mere "it" but a "you." Only "you"s and "I"s can be in relationship. A "you," however, is really just another "I." When we objectify other people—through all the prejudices and social injustices of sexism, racism, ableism, colonialism, and more—we rob others of their subjectivity. Our subjectivity is expressed most explicitly in speech. I do not mean this just in the sense of discourse in particular languages such as Thai, German, or Spanish. Consider how people feel in the presence of an awesome work of art or even a spectacular view of nature. Sometimes people will say "This song speaks to me" or "The universe is telling me something." That is, the way in which we build relationships between you and I is through speaking with one another. To objectify someone is, ultimately, to rob them of their voice. A text, rather than being a mere artifact like a book that can be put on or taken off a shelf, is a subject, a voice that has something to say. Texts speak. Books do not.

Consider some implications of this distinction. Let us say we are in a course together where we are reading Plato's masterpiece *On the Just*, which has come to be called *The Republic*. Each of us has our own different physical book, whether hard copy or digital. We read the same text, however. The text is what *On the Just* says, and we can really tell what it has to say only by listening to and understanding what is said, not just looking at ink on a page or hearing a bunch of sounds in an audio book. That is, books can be felt, seen, or even smelled. They are physical items of perception, even if they are on an Amazon Kindle or iPhone. Texts, though, exist only in the field of understanding. As we proceed together, I want us to keep a rigorous hold to this distinction. We do not write books, but book-length texts! We interpret texts, not books. Interpretation is not a matter of sensory perception, but a matter of understanding. Moreover, where do interpretations exist? In consciousness, in our understanding, not in or among material items themselves. This is not to say that two people cannot have different interpretations. It is that the difference of interpretations is of a different order than the difference of two artifacts. That is, two different texts are of a different order than two different books. For there to be a difference of interpretation, such as a conflict or competition of interpretations, these need to be of the same text, though you and I might be holding different books in our hands. Hopefully this distinction is starting to feel obvious, and you may even be wondering why I draw this all out so much. It is because in ordinary conversations, we do not keep these words this technical. Throughout this text, though, let us agree to use them as technically as possible for the sake of developing our theory about interpretation.

Scaffolding Semiotics, Semantics, and Hermeneutics Helps Isolate the Role of Interpretation

Forging a distinction between books and texts helps us specify that interpretation is something we do with texts and not something we do to books. A further set of distinctions among scientific approaches to or ways of studying language will help us isolate interpretation from related yet distinct dimensions of understanding texts. These approaches have come to be called semiotics, semantics, and hermeneutics, and we can coordinate these three by scaffolding them. We will identify the main items of analysis for each area of study, and what these different sorts of analyses yield. Let us start with semiotics.

In both popular culture and in academia—especially in the Humanities and Human Sciences—a peculiar method of analysis has risen to overall dominance and popularity called semiotics. Semiotics is the study of signs, from road signs to giving someone the middle finger, and even to names standing in for our commitments when we use our signature. In a semiotic analysis, we examine the conventions of relations among "signifiers," "signifieds," and "referents." Signifiers are those written marks, signed (such as in ASL) expressions, or spoken sounds that function as sorts of pointers. For example, the stop sign or the direction arrow on a road are signifiers. Someone standing with their arms crossed—the crossed arms might be a signifier. Even emoticons and emojis are signifiers. Signifieds, alternatively, are what people have in mind with their signifiers. That is, without the broader social convention of using red octagons to indicate drivers should stop, the stop sign would not really be a signifier. Signifieds are the intent with which we imbue signifiers. When I cross my arms standing nearby someone else, I might be expressing my mental state of discomfort or seeking to distance myself from this other person. In addition, some signifiers and signifieds are representational, and so point to a referent or purportedly real object or item in the external world. For instance, when someone sends a text message to me using a laughing face or crying face, I often assume that they are using the emoji to represent their actual face in the state of laughter or tears.

The linguist Ferdinand de Saussure coined and originally defined the semiotic field. The pragmatist philosopher Charles Sanders Pierce developed and refined it. The poststructuralist philosopher Jacques Derrida made the method *en vogue*. Due to their efforts and others, semiotics has come to be a major contender for the fundamental discourse of intelligibility in the academy, often alongside of and in collaboration with Marxism, Historicism, and other methods and theories (see, for example, Danesi 2016). That is, many scholars assume that until you perform a semiotic analysis, you have not sufficiently explained your topic of study and uncovered hidden or unconscious ideologies affecting your topic of study and your study itself. We could perform, for instance, a semiotics of peacock mating rituals through an analysis of their feather displays as signifiers. Semioticians have traced oppressive power dynamics through rhetorics of signs, such as various signifiers of white supremacy (see Yancy 2000; Urciuoli 2011). The point here is that semiotics is a crucial area of study and criticism.

Semiotics, however, is incomplete with regard to other dimensions of language and understanding (see Ricoeur 1976). We can learn to manipulate and process signs without understanding their meanings. I can parrot back to someone phrases that they teach me to sound out in an unfamiliar language, and I can even perform the sounds in contexts where they would be useful, yet I still do not hear the language as making sense, as speech. This is why we can distinguish semiotics—the study of signs—from semantics—the study of complete thoughts or sentential meanings (see Scharlemann 1981, 112). I can say something without understanding what I am saying. Whereas the focal point of analysis in semiotics is the sign or signifier, the focal point of analysis in semantics is the sentence or clause that has a subject, a predicate, and—at least implicitly—a copula. That is, sentences are the coordination and combination of multiple signs. While we might be tempted to perform semiotic analysis of sentences, we would then be treating sentences as just bigger labels or signs. The synthesis of signs into sentences generates a new entity, a complete thought or sentential meaning. A complete thought is not a signifier, signified, or referent. Thus, sentences are of a different order than signs and so require a different kind of analysis.

Semantics is the study of sentential meanings or complete thoughts. Reflecting back to basic grammar textbooks from elementary school, complete thoughts consist of both a subject and a predicate or a noun and a verb. These two are the fundamental particles of complete thoughts. The sentential subject or noun is that about which we have something to say, and the predicate or verb is what we have to say about the subject (see Dickman 2021a; Ricoeur 1976). Sentential subjects are terms like proper names, pronouns, definite descriptions, indexicals, and more. The function of subjects is to pick out some single thing from an undifferentiated background. It picks out the topic about which we have something to say. Subjects answer the question: "What is being talked about?" Even to be able to speak about something or someone, we "subjectify" them in this sense of isolating a topic. We must be careful here, however, because of our propensity toward objectification of people, to treat someone as a mere thing. Or consider speaking about something abstract, such as "love." If we say the complete thought, "Love is a battlefield," we know that "love" is not a mere object even though we treat it that way to talk about it. Treating something abstract as a concrete or specific object is called "reification," something that happens all the time to the point where we often misrecognize when we are doing it (see Bell 2009). When we misrecognize we are reifying something, we are prone to take our heuristic as if it is how things really are, that our representation is how things must be.

Predicates are what we have to say about a subject. Predicates are really where complete thoughts take on their importance and create the advance beyond signifiers, signifieds, and references. They are the distinctive trait of complete thoughts. Individual signs are building blocks for meaningful language, of course. We might even believe that signs, like names, are the starting point for language. Single words, like signs, are defined in dictionaries, and these lexical entities are potential instances of living language. However, it is in the predicative use of words, where we actually predicate of a subject in a specific moment, that language gets traction between us in conversation. Dictionaries display potential meanings of signs, but conversation—where we predicate of subjects—is where language has actuality. Words transform—or decompose, really—into signs when they are placed in dictionaries. As hermeneutic philosopher Paul Ricoeur puts this:

> Are not words lying quietly in our dictionaries? Certainly not. There are not yet (or there are no longer) words in our dictionaries; there are only available signs delimited by other signs within the same system by the common code. These signs become words charged with expression and meaning when they come to fruition in a sentence, when they are used and take on a use value. Of course they come from, and after usage fall back into, the lexicon; but they have real meaning only in that passing instance of discourse we call a sentence.
>
> (Ricoeur 1998, 35–35)

Actual words happen in use, their use in complete thoughts. When learning a new language, this difference between mere signs and living words is palpable. As long as we take each foreign term and translate them into our familiar language, we are not yet using the new language's words *as words*. It requires fluency to predicate of subjects without term-by-term or sign by sign translation.

A staple distinction in semantic content is between "reference," the *what* ostensibly indicated by a sentential subject, and the "sense," the complete thought embodied in the sentence itself including both a subject and a predicate (see Ricoeur 1976, 12-13). Complete thoughts are the "sense" of sentences uttered, signed, or written.

They synthesize sentential subjects, which enact the identifying function of language, and predicates, which enact the elucidatory function (see Ricoeur 1976, 19). The sense of statements is the new entity generated by the synthesis and is the aim of semantic analysis. The referential and identifying function, however, is why many scholars are tempted to reduce semantics to semiotics. Most people tend to reduce questions about "the meaning" of something to the referential dimension of discourse, where we tend to look for what the sentential subject indicates. That is, reference dominates as the "true" or normative definition of meaning. For example, in translations of the philosopher of language Ludwig Wittgenstein's *Philosophical Investigations*, the German term *Bedeutung* always is translated as "meaning" when what it literally denotes is "reference" (see Wittgenstein 2009). The feminist philosopher Luce Irigaray criticizes this drift toward reference away from sense as freezing the flow of lived experience, where we subordinate significant moments to our immediate capitalistic needs (Irigaray 2002, 40).

Whereas semiotics examines single signs and the broader contexts of relevantly interrelated signifiers, and whereas semantics examines combinations of signs into complete thoughts and the broader contexts of relevantly interrelated sentences, these two are incomplete and need a further scaffold for comprehensive understanding and interpretation of texts. Hermeneutics, or theories and practice of interpretation, names this additional scaffold. Texts are the combination of multiple complete thoughts. Stated simply, a sentence is a pile of signs, and a text is a pile of sentences. However, unlike signs synthesizing into the new dimension of complete thoughts, complete thoughts do not synthesize into a new entity of a text. Instead, we coordinate relevant relations of complete thoughts through concatenation, not synthesis. Concatenation is the process of identifying or creating relevant interconnection between a series of sentences (see Ricoeur 1995; 2003). Texts are concatenations of sentences into "genres." Hence the need for interpretation.

My text is all about interpretation, and thus about hermeneutics, so we will suspend further discussion of the three scaffolds here. For now, let us keep rigorously technical about these three scaffolds and their proper terms. Signs submitted to semiotics yield signifieds (and even references). Sentences submitted to semantics yield meanings or—in other words—complete thoughts. Texts submitted to hermeneutics yield interpretations. We often use the word "meaning" in all sorts of ways, as synonymous with reference, sense, signifieds, interpretation, and more, often clouding elucidating distinctions. For the rest of this text, let us try to reserve the term "meaning" for what we understand when we grasp the sense of a sentence. That is, meaning is proper to the domain of semantics, not semiotics or hermeneutics. And let us try to reserve the term "interpretation" for what we understand when we grasp the interrelation of sentences in a text. That is, interpretation—not meaning—is proper to the domain of hermeneutics, not semiotics and semantics. We do not grasp the meaning of a text, but only grasp the meaning of a sentence. A text is a compilation of complete thoughts, but a book is a pile of sentences. That is, a book is a text perceived, and a text is a book understood. It takes questions to transform sentences seen into meanings understood. It takes active reading with questions to transform a book into a text. This emphasis on the role of questions in understanding will become more pronounced as we proceed.

Chapter Summaries

To conclude this Introduction, I will provide brief abstracts for each of the following chapters to clarify the terrain we will cover throughout the rest of this text together.

Chapter 1, "The Predicaments of Interpretation," will examine the situation or predicament of interpretation. Why do we interpret at all? How do we know when we have interpreted rather than, say, explained something? What determines the "correct" interpretation, if there is such a thing as correct or incorrect interpretations? This last question forms the core of this chapter. We will see that previous attempts to address the question have isolated three primary options: the writer's intention, the reader's response, or the text itself. I propose, alternatively, that questions take priority in interpretation, which will relate to semantics as we noted above. It takes a question to transform a sentence perceived into a complete thought or sense understood. This chapter also surveys a number of contestations in the hermeneutics of sacred texts, frameworks that go beyond the writer, reader, and text, such as broader historical context, the establishment of (in)complete canons, literary genres, and more. In this light, another topic that informs the situation or predicament of interpretation is the location of the humanities in differentiation from natural sciences and fine arts in academia.

Chapter 2, "The Initiatives of Interpretation," will turn to an analysis of the mindset or consciousness of interpretation. This turn reframes interpretation, not in terms of its objects (namely, texts), but in terms of the subjectivity of interpreters themselves. The philosopher Edmund Husserl's idealist phenomenology will help us unlock interpretation as a mode of consciousness structured by intentionality. Through this, we can achieve a level of self-consciousness or reflexivity about the predicament of all interpretive consciousness. Because consciousness is structured by history and culture, all interpretation is correspondingly structured. The structuring of interpretive consciousness is detectable in identification of prejudices and examination of the nature of prejudice. This will also require some examination of the subject position of colonialist Eurocentrism.

Chapter 3, "The Mediums of Interpretation," will examine the medium in which interpretation takes place: language. We will develop a philosophy of language informed by the art and practice of interpretation. This turns our attention away from language systems (such as Thai, Arabic, English, etc.) and toward living dialogues, conversations that we actually have with one another even if we speak different languages and have to muddle through to reach an understanding. We will look at ways language transforms experience, from sensation of material environments to conceptions of meaningful worlds. Language liberates us from the immediacy of environments. In this way, language is like an artwork. The transformative power of works of art provide a clue to grasping how language liberates us, despite common figures of speech that "language" is too limiting for grasping profound truths.

Chapter 4, "The Objects of Interpretation," turns to a theory of written texts, expanding on our discussion above where we distinguished books and texts. This involves examining how writing transforms discourse in a way that spoken and signed languages do not. Through writing, we can communicate across space and time in ways speech does not allow, but we can also build worlds for imaginative exploration and transformation of our immediate experiences and perceptions. For example, are we facing forward, or North, or toward Mecca? Moreover, we will refine the priority of questioning in interpretation to specify the logic of question and answer in relation to specific sentences composing texts. Questions help us weave lines of the text into a broader fabric of meanings or an interpretation. One notion in particular shapes how we have received texts over time is the "classic," texts that have the power to continue to speak to future generations of readers.

Chapter 5, "The Practices of Interpretation," examines the social aspects and institutional elements of interpretation. How do communities of readers establish and change canons of acceptability for some interpretations and not others? How do different interpretive communities incorporate critical perspectives such as Critical Race Theory, Crip Theory, Feminist Criticism, and more? We will detail the fundamental steps of the hermeneutic arc: from initial guess, to critical explanation, to a culminating comprehension. The process and dynamism of interpretation involves all of these but grasping this involves distinguishing interpretation from explanation and clarifying existential appropriation and application.

In the Conclusion, "What Lies beyond Interpretation?," I end this critical primer by investigating and proposing roles for interpretation in the academic study of religions. There have been numerous attempts in Religious Studies to negotiate the proper place of philosophy in the intrinsic interdisciplinarity of the field. Can philosophy contribute to the evaluation and assessment of first order religious discourse as well as second order Religious Studies criticism? I end by reiterating rigorous limits of understanding and interpretation, keeping clear that everything is not and cannot be treated as a text. Although we might desire to smear meaning and understanding across everything conceivable, the end goal here is to restrain our desire for absolute understanding.

Chapter 1

The Predicaments of Interpretation

Can an interpretation be either correct or incorrect? Instead, are interpretations more or less accurate, more or less valid? If so, what determines the correctness, accuracy, or validity of an interpretation? These topics have been addressed in different ways, but the options for response have consolidated around three main proposals. Some hold that solely the writer's intention serves to establish the correctness of an interpretation. Others hold that readers take over from writers in their establishment of acceptable interpretations. Still others seem to isolate the text itself as the principal factor establishing proper interpretations. How so? How do each of these work in our navigation of interpreting texts? What assumptions do these make and what are their limitations? Are there still further options for coordinating the interpretive process? What makes these questions so significant is the precarious status of the Humanities in the broad divisions of higher education or the academy. Whereas fine arts produce films, poems, paintings, and more, and whereas natural sciences produce advances in medicine, technology, agriculture, and more, it is not clear or obvious what the humanities produce. Many humanities specialists will advocate that they help people learn critical thinking skills. This is, however, pretty vague, and also suggests that fine arts and natural sciences do not engage in critical thinking—which is false. Perhaps hermeneutics or interpretation theory can address the precarity affecting the humanities.

For this chapter on the predicaments of interpretation, I want to argue for a few things. We will examine the three main options proposed for addressing what determines the correctness of interpretations: the writer, the text, or the reader? Perhaps the default answer most people take when considering the question for the first time is to give privilege to the writer as having priority. We will also note a number of shortcomings for all three options. For example, one worry about readers taking the privilege to determine the meaning of a text is that readers can arbitrarily make texts say whatever the readers want the text to say. Alternatively, I advocate for the hermeneutic priority of questioning in interpretation. This is an option overlooked by many theorists of interpretation but is often implicitly assumed. Given the hermeneutic priority of questions, I point out ways we might support the humanities to address the precarity affecting it in the broader divisions of higher education or the academy. Cannot all disciplines and fields be defined by their proper questions? Let us turn to typical options for establishing the correct meaning of a text.

Three Major Contenders Vie to Be the Criterion for Determining the Correct Interpretation of Texts

Scholarship on interpretation tends to consolidate around three main options for determining whether an interpretation is correct or not. Is an interpretation legitimized by accuracy to a writer's intention in composing a book? Or is an interpretation legitimized by a reader's reaction to engagement with a text? Or, still further, is an interpretation legitimized by the composition itself, where the text itself determines its own meaning? Let us start with the writer's intent. As I am writing this, I have a specific plan in mind for which arguments I want to make and a specific hope for what I want readers to get out of engaging with this text. If an interpreter tells me or others that I made a completely different argument or get something completely different out of this text than what I want, then it seems pretty clear that their interpretation is incorrect. For example, in this chapter, I will ultimately argue that questioning has priority over the three major options, but if an interpreter claims that I argue for the reader's reaction then their interpretation is incorrect. Or if an interpreter says my text is a secret map to a hidden treasure, their interpretation is incorrect. My point is that prioritizing the writer's intention as the principal criterion for legitimizing an interpretation seems to be convenient, straightforward, and reliable.

A number of scholars prioritize writers' intentions in their theory of interpretation or their hermeneutics. The literary critic and scholar of education E.D. Hirsch, for example, argues that the point of interpretation is "validation," that is, the accumulation of evidence from the text, from the writer's life, and from culture should support an interpreter's interpretation (Hirsch 1967). An interpretation, according to Hirsch, is a hypothesis or a probability judgment (Hirsch 1967, 175). He names the process of determining the probability of a hypothesis through accumulating relevant evidence "validation" (Hirsch 1967, 171). The interpretation is a hypothesis because, like the scientific method in general, we test the hypothesis against the text or other data. A few strategies for increasing the probability of our interpretive hypothesis are narrowing the genre or class, identify the largest number of members in the class, and determine the frequency of similar traits across members of the class. The major criteria are relevance of the evidence and the weight of the evidence. Unlike the method in the natural sciences, where the field of relevant and weighted evidence comes from a domain of nature such as biology or chemistry, the relevant and weighted evidence comes from the text itself, the writer's biography, and the broader cultural context.

Not only ought readers grasp writers' intentions, readers also ought to relive or achieve a state of empathy with the writers. This is described more conveniently in contemporary interpretations of paintings or music. I want not only to know what was going on in Beethoven's or Chopin's mind but also to feel what they felt in expressing their feelings through their music. When I listen to George Clinton and Parliament/Funkadelic, I am moved by it. I cannot help but move my body to it. We can apply this same structure to experiencing poetry, novels, and even arguments. The goal is not merely to grasp what is said, but to feel as if the author really gets us or to feel moved by the author. This approach was promoted and developed in modern hermeneutics, with the father of romantic hermeneutic theory Friedrich Schleiermacher and his follower Wilhelm Dilthey (see Schleiermacher 1977; 1978; Dilthey 1972; 1988). For Schleiermacher, the goal is to understand the author better than they understood themselves (see Schmidt 2006, 18). An interpreter's goal is the empathetic reconstruction of the writer's experiences, aiming in particular at the writer's original thoughts and motivations or the principle that moved the writer. They believe this is possible for an interpreter because, as Dilthey explains, individual self-expressions fit within the broader context of the externalization of the human spirit, such as with laws, government, economics, religion, and more (see Mueller-Vollmer 2000, 155–156). The individual's self-expression always occurs within this broader common order, and that order is the interpreter's path of access to the writer's intentions and experiences. The highest success for an interpreter in this approach is transposition into the writer's world, recreating and reliving their experience.

The ultimate aim of this approach, taken up and emphasized in confessional or religious hermeneutic theory, is to acquire knowledge of a god's intentions for readers. These sacred writings are, after all, "the word of God"—as many people refer to their religious texts (see Plummer 2010). This compounds the required effort to grasp the writer's intention because there are technically two authors and so two separate but related intentions: the writers' and those of their gods who inspire their writings. How do these two distinct voices of authority relate with one another? The Reformed philosophical theologian Nicholas Wolterstorff attempts to develop this possibility through what he calls a "double hermeneutic" (Wolterstorff 1995). The reason why it is a *double* hermeneutic is because there are two distinct layers of interpretation that have to happen. First, there is the interpretation of the specific writer, such as Paul writing his letters or Luke writing his gospel. Wolterstorff proposes "authorial discourse interpretation" as a more subtle form of writer intent as governing what counts as a correct interpretation. It is not the inner feeling and motivation, but the actions the writer performs with the words—such as commanding, requesting, informing, and more. He defines authorial discourse interpretation as the process in which "one seeks to identify and grasp [not the propositions but] the illocutionary acts that the authorizer of the text performed by inscribing, or in some other way authorizing, the words that one is interpreting" (Wolterstorff 2006, 47). Second, according to Wolterstorff, the Christian theistic god can acquire the "rights and duties" of a speaker and via this status can perform acts of commanding and promising through appropriating the discourse of the human writers. Discourse appropriation is something we all are familiar with—it is when we take responsibility for or ownership over something someone else said, such as when we say, "I agree." Wolterstorff argues that just as state officials can deputize other persons to speak for them, so can this god deputize and appropriate the discourse of the biblical writers (Wolterstorff 1995, 95–113). It is not that this god writes biblical books directly. This god enters the discourse indirectly upon appropriating—or in more traditional terms "divinely inspiring"—human writers. Since the god is the ultimate source, religious readers are really after the god's intentions for what a text means, but this takes two steps rather than just one with purportedly ordinary human writings.

In the opposite direction from the writer's intent, there is the option of what readers make of a text as the final determiner of a correct interpretation. Note that this alternative principle for determining whether an interpretation is correct is not that the reader discovers the writer's intention. Instead, readers feel empowered to say for themselves what a text means. Readers merely introspecting about their feelings toward or reactions to a text do not define this approach to interpretation, however. This is also not to say that readers can make a text mean whatever they want or whatever they feel like making a text mean. The point is not that readers are arbitrary in their imposition on a text. It is simply that the readers have the final say about whether or not an interpretation is correct. We can identify three main models for this approach to interpretation: the phenomenological, the institutional, and the critique of ideology. The most well-known, or the phenomenological model, goes by "reader-response" theory, promoted by the literary critic and phenomenologist Wolfgang Iser. According to Iser, the reader must employ a number of acceptable procedures to activate compositional tactics used in a text in order to bring about an understanding of the text (Iser 1975, 21). To be able to interpret, to be able to read, requires some fluency with or having a repertoire of literary devices, such as being able to detect allusions and synecdoche—like when someone says "Nice wheels!" about your car. The fundamental principle, for Iser, is that because an interpretation only comes about through a reader actually engaging with a text, then it is obvious that readers have the final say for what a text means. This is what he labels the "realization" or making-real of the interpretive process (Iser 1972). Basically, you cannot have an interpretation without an interpreter!

Others such as the literary theorist Stanley Fish move beyond Iser's focus on individual readers and repertoires to the institutions that govern the "acceptability" of varying reading procedures. The acceptability of an interpretation is not in the power of individual readers but reading communities and institutions that invest individuals with power. According to Fish, the conditions of acceptability of some interpretations rather than others are not "in the text" or in the writer's intention but are based in the community of readers (Fish 1980, 349). As the community changes, so do the conditions of acceptability, and thus one interpretation rejected as "incorrect" at one point in time might be accepted as a (or *the*) correct interpretation at a later point in time. To advocate for an interpretation is less about the text and writer and more about how the reader can affect the current community of readers and the institutions legitimizing some scholars as experts and dismissing other scholars as radicals or obsolete.

Going even further than Fish are those who promote the critique of ideology in interpretation, using a hermeneutic of suspicion to uncover uses and abuses of power in texts. For example, in recent interpretation of the Book of Jonah, postcolonial scholars point out that the narrative voice seems to criticize the god referred to in Jewish communities as HaShem. The authorial voice challenges the view of HaShem as a liberator. As the Hebrew Bible and Contextual Theology scholar Kari Latvus explains, HaShem blames the Jewish people and not the colonial Babylonian powers for their exile into Babylon (Latvus 2006, 188). As the New Testament Studies scholar Mitzi J. Smith explains,

> all biblical interpretation ... is political, seeking to expose oppressive ideologies in texts, contexts, and in ancient and contemporary readers and readings. This political agenda includes the debunking of respectability politics, which claims that people of color and poor people will always be treated with dignity, justice, and respect in a racialized, patriarchal, and class-conscious society *[only] when they exhibit acceptable behaviors*. Unacceptable behaviors, according to a politics of respectability, like responding to injustice or resisting and

protesting systemic racism, sexism, and violence from authority figures, should result in negative, harmful outcomes, particularly when the actors are persons of color.

(Smith 2017, 65; my emphasis)

As I have elaborated in more detail elsewhere (Dickman 2022a, 172–174), respectability politics subordinates people to the norms of white patriarchal capitalism. Any deviations are punished brutally or eliminated. Particular attention needs to be paid to the voices of the oppressed—even at the cost of what may seem to be crucial elements of sacred texts. For example, Smith advocates overturning parables that emphasize the interests of enslavers and the purported foolishness of virgins (Smith 2017, 77–93). As the womanist homiletics scholar and reverend Raquel A. St. Clair emphasizes, interpretation of religious texts must take into consideration unique issues faced by African American women in particular (St. Clair 2007, 59; 2008, 11). Through grounding interpretation in the concrete reality of Black women's lives, the ideal is to develop a hermeneutic of wholeness supporting spirituality of all people.

Between writers and readers there seems to exist the text itself. This is the third option as a major contender to what or who has final say in determining whether an interpretation is or is not correct. Rather than the writer's intention or readers' responses, the text itself has the final say about its meaning. Ricoeur refers to this capacity of texts to speak for themselves as "semantic autonomy" (Ricoeur 1976, 30). What is "semantic autonomy"? On the one hand, texts exceed the imaginative capacities and intentions of writers by speaking to ever-further generations of readers. No writer can completely anticipate and control what their texts might come to mean. As the hermeneutic philosopher Hans-Georg Gadamer writes,

> If by the meaning of a text we understand the [writer's intention], that is, the "actual" horizon of understanding of the original Christian writers, then we do the New Testament authors a false honor. Their honor should lie precisely in the fact that they proclaim something that surpasses their own horizon of understanding—even if they are named John or Paul.
>
> (Gadamer 1977, 210)

For this approach centered on texts themselves, interpreting cannot involve the mere recovery of a writer's psychology. It is not about just repeating or merely empathizing with what the writer intends, but about understanding what the text says. The text, what is said in a book, separates from the writer's intention. It stands independent from the writer. However, the text is also autonomous from readers' interests and projections, where readers cannot take complete control to make a text say whatever readers want. Because a text speaks, there is then a speaker, a "thou," who merits readers' respect. As philosophical theologian David Klemm explains, "In this vein ... texts can manifest a subjectivity quite separate from that of their [writers] and thereby assume a voice of their own ..." (Klemm 2008, 62). This subjectivity deserves the same respect we should show to people face-to-face.

We will go into more detail about the approach centered on texts themselves, but for now I want to simply recap that we have glanced at the three main contenders for addressing what justifies an interpretation: the writer's intent, the reader's response, or the text itself. Let us turn to look at shortcomings of each of these options.

Each of the Contenders Have Shortcomings

Some people worry that choosing a criterion other than the writer's intent for determining whether an interpretation is correct will lead to readers capriciously making a text say whatever they feel like making it say (see Plummer 2010, 128–129). Wolterstorff calls reader caprice the "wax nose" problem, where interpreting religious texts, he writes, "is directly at the mercy of the vagaries of human belief" (Wolterstorff 1995, 226). In contrast, the literary theorist Roland Barthes often is described as celebrating the "death of the author" to justify reader (mis)readings (see Barthes 1977). Some scholars of Barthes's work have urged hesitancy here since he probably is using performative irony (see Carlier 2000). Barthes is, after all, a writer who is interpreted as saying that the author is not the final arbiter of correct interpretation! Fish seems more aligned with the death of the author orientation to interpretation, rejecting the writer's intent as the final criterion for correct interpretation. He writes, "no reading, however outlandish it might appear, is inherently an impossible one" (Fish 1980, 347). And the text itself is an abstraction. All texts exist in broader personal, social, political, historical, and global contexts. The point is that there are shortcomings to all three options.

Following Ricoeur, each shortcoming can be clarified as a hermeneutic fallacy. In logic and reasoning, fallacies are missteps where the validity of an argument or the truth of a conclusion goes awry (see Dickman 2021a, 94–95). Consider the valid argument form of *Modus Ponens* or affirming the antecedent:

Premise 1. If p, then q.
Premise 2. p.
Conclusion. Therefore, q.

We can provide a substitution instance of this in ordinary English as follows:

Premise 1. If it is raining outside, then the road is wet.
Premise 2. It is raining outside.
Conclusion. Therefore, the road is wet.

Most people fluent in English know that this conclusion follows from the two premises. In fact, most can make this inference without explicitly thinking about it. This is similar to how people cannot resist completing the "Shave and a Haircut" knock or saying, "Who's there?" after someone sets up the "Knock, knock!" joke. With sufficient training in reasoning, we can make inferences to conclusions from premises nearly immediately. Fallacies, though, happen when reasoning does not use valid argument forms. Consider the logical fallacy where we affirm the consequent:

Premise 1. If p, then q.
Premise 2. q.
Conclusion. Therefore, p.

We can provide a substitution instance of this in ordinary English as follows:

Premise 1. If it is raining outside, then the road is wet.
Premise 2. The road is wet.
Conclusion. Therefore, it is raining outside.

We can tell that this argument is not reliable because the road could be wet from an ice cream truck spilling its contents, a fire hydrant leaking, or any other number of reasons besides rain. In fact, we can go so far as to say that fallacies *look* like instances of reasoning but are not actually instances of reasoning. Fallacies look like arguments but are not arguments (Dickman 2021a, 95).

Just as we can make mistakes in reasoning, so can we commit fallacies in interpretation. There are three major hermeneutic fallacies, where we do something that *looks* like interpretation but is not actually interpretation. The first fallacy is the intentional fallacy, where identifying a writer's intention is taken as the ultimate criterion for settling the meaning of a text (see Ricoeur 1976, 30). For example, Thich Nhat Hanh wrote the book *Living Buddha, Living Christ* with the intention to explain ways Buddhists and Christians can get along. But is that the end of it? Is reading his book and correctly interpreting it simply a matter of figuring that out? The point here is that even if we have identified and specified the writer's intention, that is not the final step of a complete interpretation. While it might serve preliminary purposes, it does not provide us with a significant interpretation. The writing-reading relation is not a mere modification of the speaking-listening relation. Instead, what is written dislodges from the psychology and control of the writer, and so the text means more than what the writer could intend (see Ricoeur 1976, 29). As Ricoeur writes, "The text's career escapes the finite horizon of its [writer]" (Ricoeur 1976, 30). Hermeneutics, or the process of interpretation, is not psychology, using psychological tools to get at the mindset of a writer. When we interpret, then, we need to resist settling the matter just by appeal to a writer's intention.

Another fallacy is what Ricoeur calls "the fallacy of the absolute text" (Ricoeur 1976, 30). He believes this is the symmetrical inverse of the intentional fallacy. It is where a text is treated as an authorless artifact. It reduces texts to books, closer to natural non-human made objects. It is as if we find texts standing alone, like finding seashells along the shore. As I emphasized in the Introduction: books are objects, mere things. These can be put on and taken off the shelf. Books can be burned. Texts, on the other hand, cannot be burned, but only understood and interpreted. Interpretation of texts, Wolterstorff argues, is not merely an operation performed on artifacts, but a mode of engagement with another speaker. Others hold, so he claims, "that it is just the [book] we are dealing with when we take the *Proslogion* in hand and interpret. I hold that we are engaging Anselm" (Wolterstorff 2006, 36). Just for clarification, Anselm is the writer of a book titled the *Proslogion*. Wolterstorff seems to believe that only if readers engage writers can books be said to belong to the moral community, or—what amounts to the same thing—the human universe of discourse. He writes, "If the interpretation that most of us perform most of the time consists of engaging a person rather than just doing something to an artifact, then the issue arises of whether we have engaged that person justly, charitably, honorably, and the like" (Wolterstorff 2006, 49). The point here is that a text is related intrinsically to an author. My point, however, is we should not confuse the author with the writer because reading is not analogous to listening in a face-to-face dialogue. This is obvious especially in cases where the writer has died and cannot come to the service of their words. When we interpret, then, we also need to resist settling the matter by appeal to some abstract notion of books.

The third fallacy is what we can call the fallacy of reader caprice. This fallacy falls short of interpretation because it takes a reader's reaction to or feelings about text as the final solution. It is as if how a reader feels about a text is enough to say that the reader has interpreted the text. On a broader scale, if a community of readers is imbued with sufficient authority and institutional power, then whatever the institution says a text means is just what it means. If a specific feeling is all we need properly to interpret a text, then we can bypass the text altogether by inducing the feeling in readers with pharmaceuticals or narcotics. If a specific institutional power can dictate what a text means, then we can bypass reading altogether by waiting for their pronouncement—like waiting on a priest to tell me what a scripture says. There are relevant differences between reacting to a book and the work it takes to read and interpret a text, such as the effort of active questioning. When we interpret, then, we need to resist settling the matter by appeal to how a reader feels about a book or what an institution dictates that a text says.

What makes these interpretive fallacies is when we take them as final criteria for complete interpretations. This does not mean writers, readers, and texts are irrelevant for interpretation. They can be helpful as long as we keep them in their proper place. A text speaks to an interpreter, Gadamer explains, and this does not depend on the contingencies of the writer and the writer's original readers (see Gadamer 2013, 307). This historical situation of the interpreter here and now is part of what co-determines interpretation of a text. If we frame interpretation as a psychic transposition from one person (writer) to another (reader), we miss what is all involved in understanding and interpretation. As Gadamer writes, "The horizon of understanding cannot be limited either by what the writer originally had in mind or by the horizon of the person to whom the text was originally addressed" (Gadamer 2013, 413). It may sound reasonable to accept as a hermeneutic principle that interpreters should never put into a text what the writer and original reader could not intend. It only applies in boundary cases where fluent understanding and interpretation break down. Texts are not mere subjective expressions. This psychologizes texts. The writer, reader, and text are abstractions and idealizations. Who is a legitimate member of, say, the original audience? How can we draw the line between original readers and contemporary readers in a way that is not merely expedient? As Gadamer writes, "Listeners of the day before yesterday as well as of the day after tomorrow are always among those to whom one speaks as a contemporary" (Gadamer 2013, 413). Writer intent, reader reaction, and the text itself are normative concepts, representing an "empty space" useful for understanding only on some occasions. They *can* be useful when understanding and interpretation break down.

Questioning Has Hermeneutic Priority in Interpretation

I want to propose a fourth option for determining interpretations, namely that questioning takes priority in interpretation. Questioning takes priority because it is only through questioning that we come to understand—and thus interpret—anything at all. How could we understand a writer's intent if we were not asking about it in the first place? To interpret a text is to understand it as a response to a question. What is the question to which the text responds? Indeed, this critical primer itself would make no sense to someone who did not have the question, "What even is interpretation, really?" As Gadamer writes, "We understand the sense of a text only by acquiring the horizon of the question ..." (Gadamer 2013, 378). At the very least, to interpret a text is to identify the topic or subject matter and to determine the major predicate or complete thought concerning that topic. To interpret in this way is to know the thesis statement in an argumentative essay or the main plot for a protagonist in a story. This complete thought holds all the other minor premises or narrative elements together in an integrated whole. It establishes a hierarchy of topics and complete thoughts where minor premises support the main point or themes support the main plot (see Ricoeur 1974). This can help explain why readers get into interpretive disagreements. One reader might identify a different main topic than another. Or perhaps readers agree on the topic but believe the text makes a different main claim about the topic. Through discussions about their conflict of interpretations, readers might realize they overlooked obvious details or realize another reader's interpretation is better because it integrates details that their own interpretation left anomalous. The readers could instead realize both interpretations have sufficient support, leaving them in interpretive abeyance between both options (see Dickman 2022a, 20). While I will specify four discrete layers of questioning's hermeneutic priority further on, I here want to elaborate in breadth how the priority in interpretation belongs to questioning.

I take the fundamental axiom of philosophical hermeneutics to be this: to understand a question is to ask it, and to understand a complete thought is to understand it as an answer to a question (see Gadamer 2013, 383; Dickman 2021a; 2022a). How do we show that we understand a question? Showing that we understand an order involves following it. Showing that we understand a joke involves laughing at it. Just like those, showing that we understand a question means asking it. In a way, we cannot help but to ask questions that occur to us. They are not really in our power, as if we can just choose to ask or not ask a question. Even if we are just considering a question internally, and not expressing it, perhaps this is out of caution or politeness (see Dickman 2021a, 52). Being caught up by a question is more of a passion than an action, a passivity more than an activity. Some people even use the phrase, "The question *strikes* me ..." Of course, in cases where we are not fluent in a specific language or are not quite sure the wording of a question, we do not understand the question. The point is that the asking of a question *is* the understanding of the question. Understanding is embodied in the asking. But also note that the question has some independence from both the writer and the reader(s).

This matters because interpretation happens only if we can *share* a question. Since questioning is not something solely in our power, since we cannot really help it, it is this passivity that makes possible asking questions together. When I hear you ask a question and I consider that question, I necessarily ask it too. That is, your question becomes my question simultaneously. It is not really your question or my question anymore; it is *our* question. In shared questioning, we transform from isolated individuals to a community of inquiry. When a reader asks the question to which a text is a response, the reader shares the question with the writer as well as with others who have tried to address the same question or related questions. Only by asking the question am I as a reader properly positioned to take the text seriously. For example, in my courses on Ethics or Greek to Arabic philosophies, I have my students read Aristotle's discussion of friendship first, where he lays out his theory of what constitutes incomplete and complete friendships. I deliberately do this early because I know many traditional college students are already asking themselves questions about whom their true friends are, where they have transitioned from their local schools to universities meeting many new people and losing touch with previous acquaintances. That is, they are already sharing the question with Aristotle, and that helps them make sense of Aristotle's theory. Without sharing the question, the theory is lost on them—not necessarily because it is too conceptually sophisticated, but because they have no motivation for and investment in the theory. It is irrelevant to them. But it is not really Aristotle's question or the students' question. It is a question for us all, belonging to us all and uniting us as human beings. By sharing a question, we can consider another person's response to the question as a possible answer.

This provides an additional clarification for the process of interpretation, how it is we come to understand specific meanings. While understanding a question involves actually asking it, understanding a complete thought or meaning is to understand it as a response to that question we are actually asking. That is, just because we perceive a sentence—whether written, spoken, signed, or in Braille—that does not entail that we understand the meaning of the sentence. It is only when we grasp the sentence as answering our question that the sentence transforms from something perceived into a meaning understood (see Dickman 2021a, 28–29). Consider how sometimes, when we get to the end of the page of a book we are reading, we ask ourselves, "What did I just read?" In such cases, we lose track of the questions being addressed on the page, so we have difficulty transforming the sentences perceived into complete thoughts understood. However, grasping a complete thought as a possible answer to a question does not necessarily entail that we appropriate that complete thought as our own answer. That is, we can consider complete thoughts or meanings without "meaning" them, without making them our own. The transformation into meaning occurs once we situate a sentence in relation to the question it addresses. Questions are how we open our bodies and minds to incorporate meanings, to consider and weigh them with regard to our questions to decide whether or not we want to make these meanings our own (see Dickman 2021a, 39). Imagine a sentence out of context from a question it addresses, such as, "They are on the kitchen counter." Out of context, it is too difficult to make sense of the sentence. However, that changes when we realize the question it addresses is: "Where are my car keys?" What the question does is hold sentential subjects and predicates in suspense, suggesting some predicates as possible or even probable attributions to the subject. Consider a different question: "What is your name?" Given all the names around the planet, this grammatically open question suggests nearly an infinity of subjects: "My name is Muhammad." "My name is Ruth." "My name is ..." And so on. Just as with sentences perceived and meanings understood, so also with books perceived and texts understood. Books transform into texts only when we understand what is written in the book as answering series of questions.

Given both the passivity of questioning that allows us to share questions and the transformative power of questions to make sense of sentences, it is via questions that we can transfer one person's meanings to another person. When I say or write something to you, and when you identify the question that what I say or write addresses, then you can consider what I say or write as a possible meaning or complete thought. You do not have to agree and make my statements your own, of course. It is simply that you can consider my meanings. They are, after all, responses to questions we are both asking. As Gadamer writes, "We understand the sense of the text only by acquiring the horizon of the question—a horizon that, as such, necessarily includes other possible answers. Thus the meaning of a sentence is relative to the question to which it is a reply, but that implies that its meaning necessarily exceeds what is said in it" (Gadamer 2013, 378). Because many open-ended questions allow for multiple responses, we do not have to accept or appropriate the first response as the one and only answer. However, even to consider a statement as a possible answer is already to have the meaning of the sentence transferred from their thinking to my thinking. Shared questions facilitate the transfer of meanings from one person to another.

By prioritizing shared questioning in interpretation, we preserve the strengths of the other contenders while avoiding the fallacies. Asking fitting questions takes priority over identifying the writer's intention. For example, if we prioritize questioning, then we cannot simply appeal to a writer's intention as the final criterion for a correct interpretation. When we consider more discrete layers of questions guiding the interpretive process in Chapter 4, we will see that literacy is our capacity to ask questions at lightning speed. One relevant point here, though, is that—of course—a reader does not explicitly ask every single question that every single sentence answers. A writer, too, does not necessarily explicitly ask oneself a question as one writes. Thus, while an interpreter must ask the question to which a text is an answer, it is possible in some or many cases that the writer did not explicitly ask the question. In other words, while the writer may have written an answer to the question, if the writer did not explicitly articulate the question to themselves then the interpreter might not be grasping the writer's explicitly articulated intentions when the interpreter grasps the right question.

Asking the right question takes precedence over readerly caprice, too. A reader who wants to understand has to ask the question to which a text responds. Such a reader cannot just project onto a text whatever they feel like making the text mean. Inasmuch as questioning is not solely in our power or our control, readers must give up their conceit of absolute control over texts. Telling someone what they are saying is degrading to them. We have to listen to what someone else has to say because they speak for themselves. The same goes for texts. Yes, in reading, the reader gives voice to the text, grafting their reading voice to text itself (see Dickman 2022a, 47–48). In this way, a reader will have their own style of sounding out the words. But getting the resonance "just right," like Goldilocks, is not a matter of how the reader feels about the text but is a matter of the objective proportion fitting for the circumstances. That is, a reader cannot make a text say just anything. We have internalized measures of proportion and use these as a guide to getting a text just right. One way is to ask the question to which the text responds. If we can identify the explicit or implicit question and consider it, then we *ipso facto* ask the question. Imagine someone holding up a copy of *The Hobbit* when I ask the question, "Where are my car keys?" Imagine them saying, "Your question will be answered in reading this text." That is, they cannot make the text answer any question whatsoever. And not just any words can answer my question.

Asking fitting questions takes precedence over the text itself in interpretation as well. While we can understand a text only inasmuch as it answers to a question we are actually asking, it is *an* answer, not *the* answer. In questions addressed by texts, these questions open up horizons for alternative responses as well. Of course, there are many questions that have "the" answer, and not just any answer will do. For example, "Where are my car keys?" I need *the* answer. I have explained in detail elsewhere how questions with one answer are reducible to commands (see Dickman 2021a; 2021b). In brief, many sincere questions or interrogatives are a subcategory of imperatives. We can transpose such questions into commands without any loss of meaning. For example, we can transpose the question "What is your name?" into the command "Tell me your name." Many philosophers of language and logicians do just this in their attempts at erortetic logics or logics of question and answer. My argument is that there are unique kinds of questions that cannot be reduced in this way. I call them "genuine questions." Genuine questions open up to a multiplicity of responses. Consider this question: What year is it, really? Given the global hegemony of colonialist Europe, many readers might be tempted to say that *the* answer is 2023 CE (Common Era). We know though that this era-dating system is tied intrinsically to Christianity, even with the attempt to secularize it. For many Buddhists, it is 2566 BE (for Buddhist Era). For many Jews, it is 5783 AM (*Anno Mundi*, for the year after creation). For Muslims, it is 1444 AH (*Anno Hegirae*, which means the year of the Hijra when Muhammad founded the community of Medina). Some might be tempted to turn to astrophysics, to dating on the basis of the universe's expansion speed. My point is that none of these are "the" answer, but only *an* answer among many options. All of them are objectively true in their own domain of discourse, so we can be incorrect about some or all of them. This goes for texts as well. The unsaid alternative responses to questions accompany the ones that are said or written. In this way, an interpretation goes beyond the text itself.

As noted, I will return to questioning when I lay out more discrete steps of questioning in the process of interpretation. I want to conclude this chapter with a discussion of how the priority of questioning helps address the precarious status of the Humanities in higher education.

The Humanities Have a Precarious Place in between Fine Arts and Natural Sciences

In the last thirty years, a growing coalition of academics have expressed worry about the status of the humanities in higher education (see Hall 1990; Pan 1998; Harpham 2009; Newfield 2009; Fish 2010). What roles do the humanities play in society? Unlike the natural sciences, the fine arts, business schools, law schools, and medical schools, many humanities programs do not have concrete artifacts demonstrating their use-value to a capitalistic society. Natural sciences and engineering often lead to technological advancement. Fine arts programs produce plays and musical masterpieces. What do programs in the humanities—such as literary criticism, the academic study of religions, and philosophy—produce? How do these demonstrate their use-value in capitalist or neoliberal systems? Neoliberalism names diverse structures that govern much of our lives, framing what we make and what we do in terms of profitability (see Biebricher 2018). Consider how business programs and business schools did not exist until the twentieth century, in response to increased industrialization and the need for specialized training in bookkeeping, accounting, and management. This parallels the emergence of psychology and sociology as academic disciplines in the late nineteenth century, where what had originally been philosophy split off into specializations modeled on the natural sciences such as biology and chemistry. Psychology and sociology are considered human or social *sciences* rather than humanities programs. That is, fields like these demonstrate their credibility in light of the natural sciences. However, we can still detect a hierarchical value in our social imaginary with the distinction between the so-called "soft sciences" and the so-called "hard sciences." Is that distinction a hard or soft scientific distinction?

Perhaps an even starker illustration of this strategy of using "science" to demonstrate credibility is the emergence of Bachelor of Science (BS) degrees and their perceived greater value than mere Bachelor of Arts (BA) degrees. Of course, business programs have BS degrees. We can witness this with traditional humanities programs, too, such as history advocating that graduates should receive a BS rather than BA on their transcript and diploma. Why is it that a business degree or an education degree is a BS, but a philosophy degree is a BA? Over the last one-hundred years, the humanities more and more have attempted to justify their use-value to society in terms of the natural sciences (see Gadamer 2013). Why is this? It is about the perceived value and symbolic capital associated with the word "science." Consider how neoliberal forces transform advocacy for justice into commercials, such as the Gillette Corporation capitalizing on the #MeToo movement in an ad criticizing toxic masculinity. Or consider the critical theorist Theodor Adorno's critique of "free time" as a parody of itself in capitalist systems: people fetishize their vacations, expecting miracles from them, and consumable pseudo-practices saturate our time off (Adorno 2003). Many educators know well the corporatization of universities, where the bottom line has priority in all administrative decision-making. Even recent developments of centers for diversity, equity, and inclusion often are mere lip service or selling points for the institution, rather than empowered positions for genuine leverage in institutional reform (see Crouch 2012).

Indeed, the word "science" often takes the place of the word "god" in many popular writings. Many popular pieces have the title, "Science says ..." In these writings, the word "science" names an entity that functions like an ancient oracle or a pulpit preacher or a Magic 8 Ball. We learn from the oracle that babies should listen to Mozart for neural development, or that science says reading makes us more empathetic people. As if we need "science" to legitimize our enjoyment of music. As if we need "science" to justify reading. We need to be cautious here, though. I am not attempting to contribute to some anti-science or anti-intellectual bias. Over the course of the COVID-19 pandemic, for example, many people in the US resisted and even protested against recommendations from the scientific and medical experts (see Dickman 2022b). This has been due, in part, to populist devotion to the fascist leadership of former President Donald J. Trump. He even called Dr. Anthony Fauci, the director of the National Institute of Allergy and Infectious Diseases, a "disaster" and other of his associates "idiots" (see Frottrell 2020). We know this cannot really be rooted in a coherently anti-science attitude, but rather in an extremist suspicion of anything approximating the "liberal elites" and associations such as higher education—to the point of dangerous conspiracies like Pizzagate. While refusing to wear masks or degrading vaccines, these same people relied on engineering, technologies, and other medications developed in contemporary sciences. I want to point out—as a brief aside—that some African Americans express hesitancy about vaccines in particular due to the history of medical exploitation and abuse, as the journalist Rebecca Skloot illustrates in her account of Henrietta Lacks (Skloot 2011). Many experts pointed out, too, the inconsistent messaging and recommendations from the Center for Disease Control and Prevention, seeming to cater to economic pressure to "get back to normal" as if there is some paradigmatic normal. The fundamental problem is not an anti-science perspective but rather an inappropriate suspicion of expertise and power, often cloaking attempts to protect systemic white supremacy and economic privilege. My point is that, even for those who object to COVID-19 pandemic measures, science is among the many authorities to whom they remain devoted. They are among the first to reject the value of the humanities; they are among the first to propose and even ratify legislation to police against humanistic liberal arts critical thinking, such as the populist persecution of Critical Race Theory.

Liberal philosophy, neoliberal ideologies, and emotivist "ethics" underlie this exploitation and distortion of science as another arm of fascist authoritarianism (see MacIntyre 1981). The populist persecution of Critical Race Theory distorts it from a critique of systemic racism permeating the US legal institution to a generic "anti-American" attack that emphasizes slavery and genocide. Yet underneath this distortion is a genuine anxiety about individualism definitive for neoliberalism and emotivism. That is, turning to structures decenters the individual. Who is free or responsible if we are all mere functions of systemic dynamics of institutions? Consider how in white fragility, many White people respond to critiques of systemic racism—such as social or economic patterns like redlining—by expressing that they themselves are not racist or that all people should be treated as individuals (see DiAngelo 2018; Kendi 2019). As the civil rights activist and critical theorist Angela Davis explains, "Since the rise of global capitalism and related ideologies associated with neoliberalism, it has become especially important to identify the dangers of individualism. Progressive struggles—whether they are focused on racism, repression, poverty, or other issues—are doomed to fail if they do not also attempt to develop a consciousness of the insidious promotion of capitalist individualism" (Davis 2016, ch. 1). The critique of individualism is crucial for antiracist work to abolish the injustices permeating systemically racist institutions (see Davis 2005).

What does this brief detour into contemporary political philosophy have to do with theorizing about interpretation? First, inordinate focus on liberal individualism or emotivism helps explain how many people default to the writer's intent as the final determiner of correct interpretation. As we saw, many previous hermeneutic theories focus exclusively on the individual writer's intent as the criteria to distinguish good from bad interpretations. We readers are supposed to relive empathetically the experiences and emotions of writers. This adds to accumulating critiques of writer-centered hermeneutics, such as Gadamer's critique of romanticism and the phenomenological critique of psychologism (see Welton 1999). Second, defining fields in terms of questioning rather than neoliberal individualism and profiteering off of "science" can stand as a corrective to this bureaucratic lobbying for supremacy and capital. As Gadamer emphasizes, the logic of questioning is definitive for the humanities (Gadamer 2013, 378). Just as asking a question is necessary to transform a sentence perceived into a complete thought or meaning understood, and just as interpreting a text requires asking the question(s) to which it responds, academic disciplines and fields are principally defined by questions. They are fields of inquiry, and contributions to the field truly can be grasped only by asking the questions to which the contributions respond.

The ideal aspiration of the liberal arts is the curation, maintenance, creation, and interpretation of the crafts of free people (see Dickman 2020). Many college and university administrators avoid using "liberal arts" due to political polarization between liberals and conservatives, instead saying their institutions prepare students to respond to "complexity, diversity, and change ..." (Harper 2015, 31). What such administrators miss is that the liberal arts cultivate free and liberated people. We flourish in our freedom. Schools emerged primarily for the exercise and cultivation of freedom, where the Greek word *skole* literally means "leisure" (see Bourdieu 2000, 13–18). Leisure is a privileged condition free from biological needs, environmental threats, and economic and political demands. It is in leisure that we can "take time" to ask questions and think through possible responses without distraction. It is in academic institutions that we can, as the critical sociologist Pierre Bourdieu elaborates, "deal seriously with questions that 'serious' people, occupied and preoccupied by the practical business of everyday life, ignore" (Bourdieu 2000, 14). Neoliberal ideologies focusing our attention on profitability inhibit our freedom to ask questions. Academic institutions and disciplines should serve as an antidote to these kinds of suppression of freedom. The concrete product developed by humanities programs is, essentially, free human beings.

In this chapter, I have argued that questioning has priority in interpretation as opposed to writer intention or reader reaction, and I have urged that the priority of questioning can serve as an antidote to neoliberal hegemony affecting institutions of higher learning. Let us now turn to examine the initiatives of interpretation or what I will call "interpretive consciousness."

Chapter 2

The Initiatives of Interpretation

Hermeneutics and rhetoric(s) are the inverse of one another. Hermeneutics concerns the reception of discourse; rhetoric concerns the production of discourse. We seem to live in an age that prioritizes rhetoric, where countries like the US attempt to inscribe the right to free speech but neglect to inscribe the right to listen or understand speeches made. Rarely—and perhaps never—do we see protests demanding the right to listen and understand, but many people urge the need to protect and promote free expression. We should note here how emphasizing individual freedom of expression conspires to entrench us further within neoliberal or capitalist profit-making frameworks. And, as we discussed briefly in Chapter 1 on predicaments of interpretation, overemphasis on prioritizing the writer's intention in interpretation is complicit with these frameworks. I want to take time in this chapter to examine not what we interpret but who does the interpreting. That is, I want to reorient our attention away from the things that we might want to interpret, such as the Quran or the US Constitution. I want our attention turned instead toward interpreters ourselves, or more precisely interpretive consciousness. As we noted in the Introduction, interpretation seems ubiquitous, where we are doing it all the time to everything we encounter. If that is so, however, then we are doing it unconsciously most of the time. We are not even aware that we are doing it when we are doing it. In fact, when we are made to be self-conscious about it—such as in an assignment for a class or in debates about laws—it is as if we lose our ability to interpret smoothly and fluently. Maybe that is just me! Yet any athlete or musician who knows about the yips knows that the involuntary loss of a proficient skill is usually due to performance anxiety. Becoming self-conscious about what you are doing often undermines your ability to do it. Becoming self-conscious or deliberate about interpreting seems to undermine our ability to do it.

For this chapter on the initiatives of interpretation, I want to argue for a few things. I want to bring to the foreground just how difficult it is to analyze interpretive consciousness. Subjectivity resists objectification and reification, and thus cloaks itself from direct redescription. Phenomenology—especially in its foundational development in the work of Edmund Husserl—provides one way to bring "subjectivity" into the foreground through the analysis of the structure of intentionality. Through this, we can achieve a level of self-consciousness or reflexivity about the predicament of all interpretive consciousness. I also demonstrate how this predicament of interpretive consciousness is historical, where we are affected by our personal, cultural, national, and global history in our understanding. That is, we cannot help but to have prejudices, and so our task is to work with them in such a way that they are productive of rather than inhibiting good interpretations. I argue that the most dominant problematic prejudice, the one that inhibits interpretation the most, is how many people take the Eurocentric patriarchal subject position as "normal" or neutral.

Interpretive Consciousness Deflects from its Agency to the Object Interpreted

In most ancient cultures, there was not a word for "subjectivity" as we know of it today. By "subjectivity," I do not mean how people use it to denote bias, such as when people accuse journalists of being subjective rather than objective. I also do not mean it in the way people use it to distinguish, say, the objectivity of the natural sciences from the arts, where supposedly "beauty is in the eye of the beholder." The modern notion of subjectivity emerged in Europe in conjunction with the rise of modern natural sciences, the retrieval and revival of classical humanism, the Protestant Reformation, the establishment of nation-states and colonialism, the proliferation of anti-Black chattel slavery, and liberal political philosophy (see Taylor 1989; Dupre 1993; Mbembe 2017; Dickman 2022b). The modern epistemologist and philosopher of science Rene Descartes demonstrated that the subject is the foundation on which all objective knowledge can be established (see Descartes 1998). Put succinctly, nothing can be known objectively without a subject to know it, the I who knows. According to Descartes, this opens up a metaphysical dualism with the material or extended body on one side and the immaterial substance of the mind on the other side. Since then, philosophers have been troubled by the so-called "mind-body" problem. How do these two supposedly discrete substances interact? Does the mind have causal connection to the body? For modern philosophers, attempts to answer such questions are always within the framework of modern physics and biology. These were not live questions for ancient philosophers such as Plato and Nagarjuna, though. Their concern focused more on, in Greek, "psyche" (mental activity) or "pneuma" and "thymos" (spiritedness), or in Latin "anima" (the intelligible soul), or "atman" in Sanskrit (for self-subsistent soul).

The modern subject is particularly problematic because of its complicity with sexism and racism. Feminist criticism demonstrates that the masculine subject is taken as normative, as the supposedly neutral subject position (see Hollywood 1998; Anderson 2001; Irigaray 2007). To speak or write on a topic, as the existential philosopher Simone de Beauvoir discusses, women have to qualify one's voice or preface statements by making explicit one's gender, such as, "As a woman, I believe…" (Beauvoir 1980). The masculine subject defines itself through the subordination and exclusion of feminine subjectivity. A stereotype of "the Other" defines the heart of modern patriarchy. As the feminist philosopher of religion Pamela Sue Anderson elaborates, "Man creates his gender in relation to projection of the self-same subject" (Anderson 2001, 197). The feminist philosopher and psychoanalyst Luce Irigaray explains how masculine subjectivity looks for differences or transcendence in a distorted way, where such subjects wonder if there is alien life on other planets rather than right next to themselves in the same house (Irigaray 2002, 104–120). Masculine subjectivity looks vertically to the skies for salvation from aliens and gods. This subjectivity defines itself within a reified or even illusory metaphysical world, where "nature" and "body" are already abstracted from lived embodiment. For Irigaray, without embodiment with reference to a non-abstract nature, we end up oscillating between extremes of either abstractions without anchorage in our natures or regressions to sheer animality (Irigaray 2007, 96). The masculine subject has a pretense to be the universal perspective, but feminist criticism reveals the gendered character of the I or the modern subject.

In addition, the political philosopher Achille Mbembe explains how the modern subject is racialized, structured by the anti-Black racism definitive of neoliberal capitalism (Mbembe 2017). This ideology shapes most institutionalized social and private life in terms of a means/end instrumental logic wrenched around the production of financial capital (Mbembe 2017, 3–4). As Mbembe explains the historical ties between modern subjectivity, neoliberalism, and racism, "European liberalism was forged in parallel with imperial expansion … The coming of modernity coincided with the principle of race and the latter's slow transformation into the privileged matrix for techniques of domination" (Mbembe 2017, 55). Despite Eurocentric liberalism's claims about equality and enlightened reason, their explicit and implicit racism mobilizes human differences "to stigmatize and exclude, or as a process of segregation through which people seek to isolate, eliminate, or physically destroy a particular human group" (Mbembe 2017, 55). Moreover, many modern philosophers along with Descartes, such as John Locke, espoused values of equality and human rights while simultaneously investing in slave trades and colonization. It is also well-known that African and Arab philosophers' ideas preceded the European "enlightenment," such as with the pluralism of Ibn Rushd or the rationalism of Zera Yacub (Herbjørnsrud 2017).

Given all this systemic oppression and violence in modern history, it makes sense that the subject would remain hidden. It serves the interests of those privileged by inequitable institutions to deflect attention away from genuine subjectivity to the objects in its gazes. However, there is a deeper structural element of consciousness itself that prevents us from being transparent to ourselves. Imagine a scenario like the following. Pretend that you enter the classroom for our mid-morning course, and I ask you to tell everyone the story of your morning, such as what you had for breakfast, where you stopped on your way to class, what courses you attended before joining ours, etc. In your telling of the story, there is one thing that will not appear as an element within the story: the storyteller (see Dickman 2022a; Barthes

1975). That is, there will always be a remainder between the story and the discourse, or the said and the saying (see Levinas 1998). But let us say that I try to accommodate that by then asking you to tell us the story of *you telling us the story of* your morning just a moment ago. That is, we can make the storyteller a theme at a later telling of the storytelling! Notice what still happens—even then, the new storyteller of the new story still remains absent from the content of the new story. This is supposed to illustrate the systematic elusiveness of consciousness to itself. When we try to think about ourselves, we objectify ourselves to ourselves, and in so doing miss the very subjectivity that we are after in the first place. For those with the use of vision, it is like trying to look at our own eyes while looking at something. When we turn to a mirror or photograph, we do not see our own eyes, but a reflection or representation of our eyes.

The existential phenomenologist Jean-Paul Sartre explains that we tend to transform the conditions of consciousness into an entity (Sartre 1991, 32–33). Is the "I" or subjectivity a condition of consciousness or *a thing that has* consciousness? In phenomenology, it is a condition for the possibility of consciousness. The European enlightenment philosopher Immanuel Kant lays out how the "I" or subjectivity can accompany acts of consciousness, but he does not claim that subjectivity indeed always does accompany consciousness (Kant 2007, 124). The acts of subjectivity can be inferred only from the unity or synthesis of multiple appearances, where different sides or adumbrations of bark, green leaves, dirt and roots, and more, are all unified into one tree. For Kant, the combination does not arise from things like trees themselves. The combination is our contribution, or—more precisely—the contribution of subjectivity (Kant 2007, 126–127). Sartre builds upon Kant's analysis in claiming that subjectivity really only appears whenever one recollects or remembers something personal (Sartre 1991, 44). That is, subjectivity as a topic or object of analysis only emerges through reflective consciousness. As Sartre puts it, "The consciousness which says 'I think' is not the consciousness that thinks" (Sartre 1991, 45). Indeed, Sartre goes so far as to call consciousness "nothing," literally not a thing (see Sartre 1993).

My point is that making interpretive consciousness explicit to ourselves is a difficult undertaking. As Gadamer writes, "Interpretive concepts are not, as such, thematic in understanding. Rather, it is their nature to disappear behind what they bring to speech in interpretation. Paradoxically, an interpretation is right when it is capable of disappearing in this way" (Gadamer 2013, 399). For an analogy, this is like a windshield for a car. If there was no windshield, we would not be able to see the road when driving at highway speeds—the wind pressure on our eyes and face, let alone the bugs or rain slamming into our face, would prevent us from attending to the road. Alternatively, with a windshield in place, if we pay too much attention to the windshield, such as by focusing on smudges on the inside or streaks on the outside, we also will not get anywhere because we would risk crashing. What we need is for the windshield to disappear so that we can pay attention to the road. Interpretive consciousness is like the windshield: it disappears when we successfully understand something! This paradoxical element in interpretation should not inhibit us from trying to analyze it explicitly, though.

I believe there are two primary elements of interpretive consciousness that will help us make it explicit. The first is what Husserl calls the structure of intentionality, that all consciousness is oriented or is conscious *of* something. The second is what Gadamer calls prejudice, the historically conditioned character of interpretive consciousness.

Philosophical Phenomenology Clarifies the Activity of Interpretive Consciousness via the Structure of Intentionality

Husserlian phenomenology clarifies interpretive consciousness through the analysis of intentionality. This helps us increase our reflexivity about the very agent and activity of interpretation. In order to bring intentionality into the foreground, we need to go over the three fundamental steps in Husserl's phenomenological method. The first step, what he calls the phenomenological reduction, involves employing an *epoche* or bracket where we suspend our natural or normal attitude toward our experience (Welton 1999, 64-65). We all are already familiar with this whenever we enjoy fiction. There we call it "the suspension of disbelief." If we were to sit in a theater to watch a film in the *Star Wars* series, and if we kept muttering to ourselves "that's not real" or "there's no way that could happen," then we could not enjoy the film by entering and entertaining the imaginary world placed before us. With the phenomenological *epoche*, Husserl is advocating for employing this suspension of disbelief with regard to all of our experience. This forces us to suspend our natural attitude, all the things we take for granted or as obvious in our normal way of interacting in the world (see Welton 1999, 61; Blum 2012, 1032). The *epoche* is not a form of doubt, where we negate our long-held beliefs. It is, rather, a productive effort on our part to consider an alternative world of significance. He calls this a reduction not because we are simplifying a complex phenomenon or explaining a phenomenon away, such as saying that love is just a chemical reaction in the brain. Rather, it is a reduction in the culinary sense, where we make—say—orange juice concentrate by boiling out the extra water. The reduction involves removing something, the natural attitude. More importantly, though, the reduction concentrates us on what Husserl calls "pure consciousness" (Welton 1999, 66–69).

Pure consciousness is a new region of our existence, where we can fixate on what is within or immanent to consciousness and its universal structures such as the ego, the noetic and noematic correlates, and more. The fundamental structure of consciousness itself is intentionality (Welton 1999, 70). We should not confuse intentionality with something being "intentional" or "unintentional," in the sense of where we do something on purpose or on accident. Having an intention to do something, such as a plan to go running later today, is not what phenomenologists are trying to get at. Unfortunately, in philosophy and the academic study of religions there are terms like "intentionality" that can get confused with how we commonly use related words, just like the queer theory term "performative" (which doesn't mean fake!) or the Kantian term "transcendental" (which doesn't mean transcendent or metaphysical!). Intentionality names the feature of consciousness that is object-directed, where to be conscious is to be conscious *of* something. All of our conscious processes are oriented toward or aimed at something. Yet what is this "something" at which consciousness aims? It cannot be a typical physical object, because—given the *epoche*—we have bracketed these natural objects out. Besides, these are outside or beyond consciousness anyway. When

I ask what these things are in consciousness at which it aims, I am asking about something *immanent* to consciousness.

What we should notice with our concentrated focus on consciousness itself is how the flux of consciousness coalesces into two strict poles, what Husserl names the noetic (the activity) and noematic (the thing aimed at) moments of intentionality. The noesis (singular) is the acting or the subjective pole of an instance of consciousness, whereas the noema (singular) is the action or object pole of an instance of consciousness (see Welton 1999, 93). We can see this difference in a distinction we make in ordinary conversations, such as the difference between making a statement (the noetic moment) and the statement that is being made (the noematic moment). We can isolate these poles in many domains of consciousness, such as memory or imagination. For example, take a moment to recall the last time you laughed. In this moment of recollection, we can identify the one actively doing the remembering and that which one is remembering. That is, there is the rememberer, and there is the memory. Or take moment to imagine a unicorn playing with a centaur. There is the activity of creating the scene, and there is the scene created. A structural law of consciousness or a more precise formulation of intentionality, then, is that all noetic moments have a noematic moment belonging them specifically. According to Husserl, only noesis and the hyletic movements or raw impressions are inherent in consciousness (see Welton 1999, 96). That is, the noemata (plural)—the memories, the imaginative scenes— are not part of the aiming of consciousness, but the things at which noeses (plural) aim.

It is tempting to think that noemata are just mental representations of actual objects, but for Husserl this would lead to an infinite regress where we have to make a representation of the representation, and then a representation of that representation, and so on (see Welton 1999, 90–91). Noemata are *actual* objects parenthesized or bracketed by the *epoche*—neither "things-in-themselves" nor mere mental representations or hallucinations. The noematic core is, rather, a complete thought or meaning with a sentential subject, copula, and predicate. That is, the *epoche* brings to the foreground the meaning of things rather than "things in themselves." That is, we do not need to "see" what we remember, but do need to tell ourselves the story composing them out of a series of meanings or complete thoughts. Or with imagination, we do not need to "see" what we imagine, but we do need to compose the story with a series of meanings. I want to be clear, though, that by "meaning" here we are talking about sentential meaning, or what is sometimes called a proposition, judgment, assertion, complete thought, or claim.

It is through discourse that we disclose consciousness, then. Living language is not some clothing, for Husserl, as if we can remove the clothing and get at the naked or pure contents themselves (see Welton 1999, 102). Discourse is the embodiment or concretion of intentionality (see Husserl 1973). Predicates reveal radiating aspects of the sentential subject, and copulas are a new being generated through the synthesis of subjects and predicates (see Husserl 1973, 235). The new being is a meaning (see Dickman 2016). That is, sentential subjects and predicates copulate to give birth to or produce meanings or complete thoughts. However, not all possible complete thoughts are actualized. We only think or speak of some things and not others, and we only think or speak of some things in some ways and not in other ways. Actualized complete thoughts, ones we actually think or say, are the foreground against the backdrop of broader horizons of possible meanings (see Welton 1999, 109). Like when we see a tree and say, "I'm going to climb that!" From the angle we approach it, it looks fun to climb and we judge it that way. This actual consciousness is accompanied by and includes many more possibilities for what could be or could have been. All that is unthought accompanies all that is thought. These possibilities define the horizon, our openings to further meanings and discourse.

There are two further steps in Husserl's method for phenomenology, and it should prove helpful to look briefly at these as well. The second step is what he calls the eidetic reduction, where we seek to move beyond mere stereotypes and generalizations to genuine universal concepts or the *eidos* (Welton 1999, 284). Only through universal concepts can we establish objective and reliable knowledge. However, eidetic universals or concepts are not within natural objects as if they are naturally similar, but are instead structures of consciousness. He sometimes refers to these as "essences." He is criticized as an "essentialist," as someone who projects essences on things and—more importantly—people. According to these critics, when we essentialize someone we are treating them unjustly, projecting a stereotype on them, making it seem as if there is a normal way someone should be, and any deviation is unnatural (see Ahmed 2006). This criticism, however, is not sufficiently reflexive. It inadvertently essentializes "essence" in attempting to overcome or critique our propensities toward essentializing (see also Blum 2012, 1034). It takes a substance metaphysics approach to defining "essence" when there are plenty of alternatives (see Ronkin 2009). Husserl does not seem to subscribe to a substance metaphysics, and his notion of universals within the eidetic reduction are not "essences" in the sense of substances (see Husserl 1990, 55). Instead, we should think of reduction here again in the culinary sense, such as when we get to the gravy. What we are doing when we perform an eidetic reduction involves trying to identify what Husserl calls the "invariant in the variations" (see Welton 1999, 293). That is, we examine a variety of perspectives and judgments, say, about boxing or asking questions or religious experiences. Maybe we are doing these or having these ourselves; maybe we are reading different people's accounts of undergoing them. By attending to the "invariant," we are trying to capture the gravy of boxing or asking questions or religious experiences. For example, what is necessary and universal to all sincere questions? There might not be just one thing, but a number of things. In the case of sincere questions, they all seem to require these three components: the questioner cannot know the answer, they desire to know, and they are using the question to gain that knowledge (see Dickman 2021a).

The third, and culminating step for Husserl, is what he calls the transcendental reduction (see Welton 1999, 142). For Husserl, subjectivity is what produces, constitutes, and establishes all conceptualization and therefore all objective knowledge. Just as with the other two reductions, this is in the sense of a culinary reduction, concentrating our effort to the fundamental source. As noted before, without a knower there is no knowledge. More significantly for us, without an interpreter there is no interpretation. Examination of concepts or *eidos* in the eidetic reduction uncovers "the transcendental I" (see Welton 1999, 311). For Husserl, this is the pure ego intrinsic to the very capacity for thought and action, not in specific sensations and perceptions but in all possibilities of the "I can" or capacities for meanings, thoughts, actions, and interpretations (see Welton 1999, 142; Merleau-Ponty 1968, liv). As Gadamer writes, "Transcendental subjectivity is the Ur-Ich ('the primal I') and not 'an I.' For that, the basis of the pregiven world is superseded. It is the absolute irrelative to which all relativity, including that of the inquiring 'I,' is related" (Gadamer 2013, 240). As a brief aside, the term "transcendental" should not be confused with "transcendent." Something that is transcendent is beyond our world or the ordinary world (see Dickman 2017). For Husserl, the phenomenological reduction or *epoche* resists both speculation about transcendent entities and the natural attitude that takes everything as transcendent or mind-independent. That is, we have already bracketed out everything transcendent so we can concentrate exclusively on what is immanent to consciousness. We must, Husserl writes, "exclude everything that is transcendently posited" (Husserl 1990, 4).

Many critics, following the poststructuralist philosopher Michel Foucault, dismiss Husserl as positing a transcendent or even crypto-theological origin point (see Foucault 1983; McCutcheon 1997; Hughes and McCutcheon 2022). This is a critical issue in the academic study of religions, rooted in questions related to whether an "outsider" can really understand an "insider" of a religion, especially in cases where a religious person takes their tradition as literally true to reality and a naturalist scholar takes that religion as obviously false. Scholarship and theory that smack of any covert Christian theology becomes politically and critically suspect, sneaking in Christian supremacy through the backdoor. Husserl—and phenomenology generally—is suspected of complicity with a broader theological rather than critical project. Husserl, as with others following Kant's antimetaphysical philosophy, uses "transcendental" to name immanent—not transcendent—conditions for the possibility of specific experiences or events of consciousness. Hence, phenomenology properly undertaken cannot possibly be crypto-theological. It is as against substance metaphysics and the construal of "essences" within that framework as any other sufficiently critical position developed in the twentieth and twenty-first centuries.

We should not confuse transcendental subjectivity with individualism, although Husserl's idealist phenomenology tends that way (see Ricoeur 1975; Theunissen 1984). Perhaps the better term is transcendental intersubjectivity. Rather than you or me, it is an "us." For Husserl, transcendental intersubjectivity constitutes the objective world (see Welton 1999, 145). Again, this is not some mystical or metaphysical transcendence from experience but an immanent and necessary component of experience. This does not mean that we are the same person, or limbs of some bigger or greater person like the Borg in *Star Trek*. While we each have our own perspectives, something shared by all of us is having a perspective as such. As we have learned from feminist epistemology, a perspective involves a standpoint, one that opens to a broadening horizon (see Anderson 1998). Because we have unique perspectives, we can learn from one another. What shapes our unique perspectives, though? Let us turn to examine the impacts of history on interpretive consciousness.

Interpretive Consciousness Is Situated in and Affected by History

We are not simply abstract subjectivities. We live and grow within unique circumstances peculiar solely to each of us as individuals. The existential philosopher Simone de Beauvoir explains that this is our tragic ambiguity, where we are both subjects and objects for both ourselves and others (Beauvoir 2015, 6). Intersecting social structures of privilege and marginalization establish unique contexts within which each of us try to make something of ourselves, to be ourselves, or by which we are prevented from doing so (see Weldon 2015; Cho, Crenshaw, and McCall 2013). As Beauvoir famously puts it, "One is not born, but becomes, a woman" (Beauvoir 1980). That is, society has predetermined norms for what women are supposed to be, who counts as paradigmatic for what it means to be a woman in our society. But this applies just as much to other social structures such as ableism, ageism, racism, and classism as much as sexism. For example, the existential psychoanalytic philosopher Frantz Fanon states that as a Black man in racist society, "I am made into an object even for myself, but seek to resist this thematization" (Fanon 2008, 85). Black people in particular, as well as others under marginalizing categorizations, are overdetermined from the outside, told how to be by all others—not merely by white supremacists, but by any others who have internalized racism, misogyny, ableism, or what have you.

What Fanon, Beauvoir, and other antiracists and social justice advocates demonstrate is that our individualized consciousness, our "self-consciousness," is not transparent to itself. Husserl makes it seem as if the correlates of consciousness—the noesis and noema—are transparent to one another, that we have immediate undistorted access to the meanings of which we are conscious. Both Ricoeur and Derrida critique this as a shortcoming of Husserl's phenomenology. Ricoeur, for example, explains that phenomenology must take a detour through hermeneutics—that is, language permeates consciousness in that we can never access consciousness in its purportedly "pure" form, but always through its expressions in languages. Therefore, we must interpret and not merely reflect on self-consciousness (see Ricoeur 1975). Derrida explains that the fundamental metaphoricity of language also intervenes on the purported transparency of consciousness to itself (Derrida 1973, 110–120). Consider the occularcentrism, or vision-centered, model of consciousness that permeates figures of speech in the English language. Have you ever heard someone say, "Do you *see* what I mean?"? Why is it perfectly normal and natural to use a vision metaphor for consciousness, but not an olfactory model, where it could be common to say, "Do you *smell* what I mean?"? The vision-centered metaphor is sneaky too. What else is "reflection" but the use of a mirror and our vision of reflected images as the model for some purportedly inward activity of consciousness? And this says nothing about the unconscious forces of the capitalistic economy, the Id, or the will to power identified by the masters of the hermeneutics of suspicion—the economic philosopher Karl Marx, the philologist Friedrich Nietzsche, and the psychoanalyst Sigmund Freud. That is, these forces, along with language and dynamic social structures, collide or intersect to generate fields of potential capabilities, privileges, and marginalizations.

Transcendental—not transcendent—subjectivity is distinct from the self in this way. We constitute a "self" in the midst of all these forces.

The self is what we are conscious of when we become self-conscious. As noted above, transcendental subjectivity is elusive to consciousness because it is always the agency pole of consciousness, not the meaning or "object" pole of consciousness. Does subjectivity exist? No; or, at least, not in the sense that a self does. Transcendental subjectivity is an immanent necessary condition for any instance of consciousness, even self-consciousness. In fact, multiple philosophical and religious traditions recognize subjectivity's complex interrelation with the self. For example, in classical, medieval, and modern Buddhist philosophical debates, the existence of a person's "soul" or essential substance is denied in the doctrine of *anatman*, literally "no soul" (see Loy 2013; Dickman 2016). One key element of Buddhist ontology is this rejection of an ultimate "self" (see Harvey 2009, 269). Siddhartha Gautama, the historical Buddha, called this self into question, where people take this as who they truly are. For Gautama Buddha, to identify with the self is to misunderstand reality and what a self even is. When asked directly if the self does or does not exist, the Buddha reportedly remained silent (see Strong 2002, 97). He taught that to agree to either option would be to associate with extremists—reificationists on the one hand, and annihilationsists on the other. In other words, the Buddha sought to navigate a middle way between believing the ego is the self and believing that the self is merely a function of intersecting forces. What both options share is the assumption of a substance metaphysics: either the self is some-thing, or it is no-thing. The Buddha does not deny the existence of the self but denies that which we egocentrically take to be our selfhood and the object-centered metaphysics presupposed in the questions. Nevertheless, there is no identifiable eternally existing soul, but instead there are different states of consciousness emerging or produced in different contexts.

A more fundamental feature of reality is what we can call "dependent emergence," a spin on the Sanskrit *pratityasamutpada*. This is the positive inversion of the better-known Buddhist term "emptiness" or *shunyata*, an extension of *anatman* to all things. Matsumoto Shirō, a leading representative of contemporary Critical Buddhism, tirelessly asserts that dependent emergence is the distinctively Buddhist insight and the measure of all authentic Buddhist thought (Matsumoto 1997, 166). Nagarjuna, founder of the Madhyamaka or middle-way school of Buddhist philosophy in the first century CE, defines dependent emergence by asserting the emptiness of all things (Nagarjuna 1995). This appeal to emptiness led nineteenth century European scholars to describe Buddhism as the cult of nothingness, and Nagarjuna as perhaps its ultimate priest (see Faure 2009). We now understand that rather than claiming nothing exists, Nagarjuna's point is that the way in which we ordinarily conceive of things clouds our ability to notice the fundamental interconnectedness of all things (Nagarjuna 1995, 48). As Nagarjuna writes, "For him to whom emptiness is clear, everything becomes clear. For him to whom emptiness is not clear, nothing becomes clear" (Nagarjuna 1995, 69). Without an understanding of dependent emergence and the accompanying emptiness of all seemingly substantive things, we end up grasping at and clinging to mirages. Through the principle of dependent emergence, Nagarjuna suggests that one can be released not only from attachment to particular possessions but also from exaggerated self-centeredness. As Nagarjuna writes, "From the pacification of the self and what belongs to it, one abstains from grasping onto 'I' and 'mine'" (Nagarjuna 1995, 48). Dependent emergence means that reality consists of interrelations; thus our actions, words, and our very selves are parts of greater systemic wholes. The point is that we cannot confuse our "self" with transcendental subjectivity.

On the transcendental level—remember this is not transcendent, but immanent—it is about the opaqueness of consciousness to itself. The most precise way to determine this opaqueness is through the concept of prejudice. Prejudice is distinct from bias, an unthinking affective habit in our emotional dispositions toward particular events and positions that involve unconscious refusals to consider reasonable alternatives and which result in unfair actions. Biases are emotive short cuts so we do not have to think things all the way through, which is useful since we do not always have enough time (see Dickman 2021a, 165; DiCarlo 2011, 44). Biases shape or color how we perceive the world, others, and ourselves. Prejudices, however, are more specific. As the feminist hermeneutic philosopher Georgia Warnke states, "What makes a prejudice a prejudice... [is] the way in which it orients our thinking or conscious attempts at interpretation without our attending to the character of the orientation itself" (Warnke 1997, 94).

They are, literally, pre-judgments or complete thoughts formed before examining all the details with enough thoroughness (see Gadamer 2013, 283). Recall our vigilant focus on complete thoughts, with sentential subjects and predicates. In phenomenology, again, the noema or object-pole of consciousness consists of complete thoughts or judgments. Prejudices are—or really should be—judgments of a provisional or tentative quality, and we are—or really should be—ready to revise them as we learn more. They are what we think when we anticipate what something is or means. There have been attempts in Eurocentric enlightenment thought and modern science to escape all bias and prejudice, with an aim at total objectivity. While that might be a great aspiration, we can wonder whether this is really practical or possible. Can anyone really be completely objective? Even if we think not, we should also resist the alternative extreme pessimism where we throw up our hands and say, "So no one knows what is going on! Everyone has bias and there is nothing we can do about it!" If (or since) it is true that we are all biased and prejudiced in one way or another, then our quest should not be to get rid of them but to figure out how to make use of them and live with them. To desire to rid ourselves of all prejudice is—at least inadvertently—a desire not to be human!

What we need to do is distinguish between productive prejudices that facilitate understanding and tyrannical prejudices that inhibit understanding (see Warnke 1997, 94; Gadamer 2013, 282–289). Hermeneutic philosophers identify at least three tactics for clarifying and promoting productive prejudices. The first is temporal distance (see Gadamer 2013, 309). Consider those times when we get angry. Something happens—maybe a person steps on your toe while boarding a bus—and you respond immediately with rage. It is like a reflex rather than a response. And it takes time to calm down. Once calm, you can put the accident in proper perspective. You realize the person was rushing to make sure they could help their kids board the bus. You also realize you had left your foot partially in the aisle. You can think to yourself, "It was just an accident." The time even allows you to realize you were prone to overreact because of frustration with your boss at work. That is, not only can you put the accident in context, but you can also even put your reaction in context. Whereas the immediate reaction was anger, the time allowed you to interpret the whole situation and yourself in a broader perspective. The same principle applies to historical events or books. Whereas we can tell where a specific past event fits in global history or which texts still speak to us today, it is more difficult to tell which events happening today will have lasting impact or whose voices will speak to future generations in significant ways.

The second tactic is confidence in trustworthy authorities, not simply because they have institutional power but because they reliably demonstrate superior insight (see Gadamer 2013, 292). Genuine authority is not authoritarian. When a child questions their guardians, such as when they ask why they have to go to bed and cannot stay up late, guardians or parents will often say, "Because I said so!" That is, they do not provide reasons or insight as to why their guidance is appropriate, but instead they default to their power to coerce the child's action. As Warnke elaborates, relations of domination and power distort our interpretive capabilities through which we "might test and expose the illegitimacy of [our] prejudices" (Warnke 1997, 98). Productive prejudices rooted in authority are not based on the person or institutional role, though. Instead, they are rooted in the content itself that the authority shares with us, an insight that we did not yet have. This is an experience we commonly have, such as when we express, "Oh, that's so true!" Or think of all the things you have learned from experts on TikTok. In principle, though, they can be validated independent of the authority, through one's own reasoning and investigation.

The third—and for our purposes, the most significant—tactic for clarifying and promoting productive prejudices is by asking questions. As mentioned above, noema are conceived of best as complete thoughts with subjects, copulas, and predicates. In other words, they are judgments. The thing about questions is that they *suspend* the copulation or combination of subjects and predicates (see Dickman 2018a, 236; 2021a, 39). Whereas complete thoughts or judgments are assertions, questions do not assert something—or even negate assertions by claiming the opposite. Questions hold a subject in abeyance with any number of possible predicates or hold a predicate with any number of possible subjects. For example, imagine someone asking, "Where are my car keys?" Car keys are the subject, and a number of predicates are possible: upstairs in the bedroom, on the kitchen counter, locked inside the car, etc. Or imagine someone asking, "What gets wetter as it dries?" Gets wetter is the predicate, and a number of subjects are possible: umbrellas, towels, etc. Within a question are suggestive possibilities held in suspense, none of which is an assertion or negation of an assertion. In this way, questions put prejudices at risk of criticism, making them explicit for consideration, evaluation, assessment, and more. Our hidden prejudices prevent and inhibit understanding and interpretation. Questioning exposes them. Note that this does not get rid of all our prejudices as if we can magically become completely objective. Questioning brings our prejudices into play and opens us to listening to what others have to say without necessarily taking what they say as absolutely correct or authoritarian (see Gadamer 2013, 310). However, it is our prejudices more than transcendental subjectivity that makes us who we really are. They are effects of our consciousness being affected by history. As Gadamer writes,

> History does not belong to us; we belong to it. Long before we understand ourselves through the process of self-examination, we understand ourselves in a self-evident way in the family, society, and state in which we live. The focus on subjectivity is a distorting mirror. The self-awareness of the individual is only a flickering in the closed circuits of historical life. That is why the prejudices of the individual, far more than [one's] judgments, constitute the historical reality of [one's] being.
>
> (Gadamer 2013, 289)

Our prejudices emerge from intersecting social and historical institutions. Questioning, along with temporal distance and credible authority, is how we can work with rather than work against our prejudices.

Among Productive and Illegitimate Prejudices, the Eurocentric Colonialist Patriarchal Position Is Especially Pernicious

There is one illegitimate prejudice that is especially pernicious and distorts our capacity to interpret and understand. It goes by many names: patriarchy, white supremacy, orientalism, sexism, racism, etc. To return to our earlier engagement with Mbembe, Irigaray, Beauvoir, and Fanon, I want to label it the Eurocentric colonialist patriarchal position. While this does leave out ableism, homophobia, religious discrimination, and ageism—among many others—from the label itself, these are implied structurally (see Kafer 2013; Gawande 2017). At times, one structural privilege may take precedence over others. What is crucial, though, is that this perspective takes itself as an absolute point of reference. It is not merely one point of view among others, but *the* point of view—with a pretense to total objectivity, ideological neutrality, entitled liberalism, and meritocratic authority (see DiAngelo 2011, 57). The perniciousness results from a misrecognition in which, rather than critical self-awareness of itself as one perspective among others, it purports to *be transcendent* subjectivity—not as the immanent structure of consciousness in transcendental subjectivity but as a transcendent entity or a "god's eye view" (see Anderson 2001, 195).

The claim to total objectivity emerged in the European Enlightenment and the rise of modern Western science. As Gadamer explains, "there is one prejudice of the Enlightenment that defines its essence: the fundamental prejudice of the Enlightenment is the prejudice against prejudice itself" (Gadamer 2013, 283). Modern Western science attempts to follow methodological principles laid out by Descartes and Francis Bacon, where hypotheses are formulated and data gathered to attempt to falsify them. In this way, the ideal is to rid oneself of all superstition and bias. Just as natural sciences do this with nature, the human sciences attempt to do so with culture and society. The Religious Studies scholar Tomoko Masuzawa explains how this takes shape in the 1800s with regard to the category of "religion" in particular. This is the period in which, Masuzawa writes, "the protean notion of 'religion' ... came to acquire the kind of overwhelming sense of objective reality, concrete facticity, and utter self-evidence that now holds us in its sway" (Masuzawa 2005, 2). It seems obvious that every culture has (a?) religion, and that all religions share an essential structure. This led many early scholars of comparative religions to "rank" them on a continuum spanning from disenfranchised "primitive" or indigenous traditions, to Asian polytheistic traditions, to the monotheisms of Islam and Judaism, to the consummate or "true" religion of European Christianity. We can still detect these supremacist presumptions in World Religions textbooks and Religious Studies curriculums.

Masuzawa raises the question, "How can we be sure our science or study of religion is not in collusion with malign forces in the name of pluralism with its hidden supremacist pretensions and exclusivism?" (Masuzawa 2005, 325).

This perspective also purports to be ideologically neutral, as if it can make all of its biases, prejudices, and assumptions transparent to itself. As the postcolonial critic Edward Said explains with regard to "Islam" in particular, that one's interests in a subject matter derive from our own needs and that knowledge of another culture rests on prior circumstances whereby it is brought into the foreground (Said 1997, 139). Disciplines like history, anthropology, religious studies, and philosophy normalize their object of study, and using the preferred method supposedly gets us beyond bias and prejudice. What look like "facts" are the products of general social imaginaries. With regard to Islam in particular, a state of emergency—such as concerns about terrorism—keep the "scholars" or "experts" in Islam in business (see Said 1997, 149). As Said writes, "Virtually nothing about the study of Islam today is 'free' and undetermined by urgent contemporary pressures" (Said 1997, 143). It is as if the only question Westerners really have about Islam or Muslims is whether or not they are anti-American. This pretense to neutrality is even more insidious, leading us to misrecognize differences between ideologies and worldviews (see Dickman 2022b). It serves the interests of ideologies to be confused with explicitly conscious worldviews. People casually use these terms interchangeably, such as when talking about "the Buddhist ideology." Worldviews, though, have explicit doctrines and authoritative institutions that can be directly addressed and criticized, whereas ideologies shape people's lives even if they hold to worldviews that diametrically oppose them. For example, what can we make of someone who claims to be an atheist but still believes that it is 2023 CE, a secularization of the Christian era-dating system? Ideologies are dissimulative, and thus we misrecognize their effects on us (see Ricoeur 1991; Bell 2009 108–117). Ideologies are hegemonic in that they assimilate those elements that attempt to resist them, such as with the Nike Corporation profiting off of Colin Kaepernick's protests against police brutality to African Americans. As the postcolonial theologian and critic of biblical literature Kwok Pui-Lan explains:

> The shift to the flesh-and-blood reader contests the assumption that there is a "universal" reader and an "objective" interpretation applicable to all times and places. The claim of an "objective" and "scientific" reading is based on a positivistic understanding of historiography, which presumes that historical facts can be objectively reconstructed, following established criteria in Western academia. But the historical-critical method is only one of the many methods and should not be taken as the "universal" norm for judging other methodologies. Its dominance is the result of the colonial legacy as well as the continued hegemony of Eurocentric knowledge and cultural production of our time.
>
> (Kwok 2016, 8)

The point here is that reading is never neutral, and that the presumption to neutrality is itself a symptom of a peculiar prejudice rather than somehow transcendence from all prejudice.

An entitled liberalism accompanies these other dynamics. There is a toxic need within this perspective to be admired (see Manne 2020, 18). As the feminist ethicist Kate Manne explains, this perspective is steeped with resentment, where the men who take this perspective "feel the world owes them certain favors" (Manne 2020, 27). This perspective enables, protects, and fosters bad actors. It is a "himpathetic" social system, to the point where individuals demand respect as individuals rather than as representatives of groups. This is an especially problematic characteristic of white privilege, where purportedly liberal and progressive White people claim to be "colorblind," urging the need to treat everyone as individuals. Colorblind racism, however, overlooks how Black people in the US have been marginalized systemically throughout health care, legal, and education institutions. That is, Black people do not have the privilege to claim individuality in the face of institutions that treat people according to group membership along the color line. Moreover, liberal efforts to confront these injustices fail. As the political philosopher Howard McGary explains:

> Since liberals assign great weight to individual liberty, they are reluctant to interfere with actions that cause indirect harm. So even though they recognize that living in a society that has an attitude of disrespect towards African-Americans can constitute a harm, and a harm caused by others, they are reluctant to interfere with people's private lives in order to eliminate these harms.
>
> (McGary 2003, 694)

Moreover, the entitlement is based on an assumption of individual success, as if an individual earns their position because of merit. As the feminist writer Ijeoma Oluo elaborates, although universities and colleges in the US claim to reward people based on recognition of their individual merit, the jargon of meritocracy cloaks how higher education preserves and perpetuates white male power—even if they are left-leaning politically (Oluo 2020, 97). White men tend to be promoted or praised for merely existing, let alone for talking explicitly about racial justice (Oluo 2020, 224). The point is that this perspective claims authority by virtue of its position, as if just by holding a position of power, one believes one deserves it and one believes they know what they are doing. It is the Dunning-Kruger effect on a massive hegemonic scale. Genuine authority, however, comes from superior insight and can be verified independently of the authority itself (see Gadamer 2013, 291).

What the study of transcendental subjectivity as an immanent structure of consciousness shows us is that the particularity and partiality of our points of view should not be mystified as a transcendent god-like perspective. As Gadamer writes, "We always find ourselves in dialectical tension with the prejudices which take us in and parade themselves as knowledge but which really mistake the particularity and partiality of [our] view for the whole truth" (Gadamer 1986, 59). A mere reaction to something is not an interpretation of it. As we have elaborated, neoliberalism shapes our prejudices and biases, making us prone to react in certain ways profitable for certain institutions. These systems extract profits from our reactions. Consider how the media interpret and cover "Islam" after specific events such as the hostage crisis in Iran, the destruction of the World Trade Centers, and the Syrian refugee crisis. As Said explains, these are not interpretations, but ideologues promoting propaganda to serve state and capitalist interests (Said 1997, 6–8). Fallacies, or flaws in argument forms and reasoning, can be called paralogisms, like "paranormal" names what is beyond the scope of scientific method and knowledge. So too are such "interpretations" more appropriately called "parainterpretations," reactions that are beyond the scope of interpretation. What this reveals is our need for dialogue, where we can broaden our horizons of understanding through understanding what others have to share. Dialogue is the real embodiment of transcendental intersubjectivity; it is the possibility for growing through radical differences constituting ourselves. Indeed, because of our particular differences, we require interpretation and hermeneutics. Interpretation is part of us because we are different from one another. Let us turn to these dynamics of language and dialogue.

Chapter 3

The Medium of Interpretation

We are all different from one another, perhaps radically different. Hence the need to communicate and interpret. This is the moral of the story from the previous chapter. We can approach this as an inversion of how the myth of Babel in the Hebrew Bible often is taken. Interpreters typically take the dispersion of human beings into diverse languages as a problem that needs to be overcome. The myth suggests to many interpreters that cultures are incommensurable, and that we will never find unity against a common enemy again—the enemy, of course, being HaShem for committing global genocide with the flood and the unity being humanity's shared effort at creating the tower to storm the heavens to take control. These interpretations suggest there is some transcendent point of view, some paradise of a universal language we have lost, which we need to get (back) to, such as with the creation of Esperanto in the late 1800s. As Gadamer elaborates, "this mythical account turns things on their head when it conceives of [humankind] as originally unified in using an original language later sundered by a confusion of languages" (Gadamer 2013, 460–461). There was no idyllic era "before" Babel, however. Since it is a myth, it never existed historically. As Ricoeur asks, "have we not exchanged the idea of universal truth for that of radical relativism?" (Ricoeur 2010, 37).

What these takes on the Babel myth neglect, however, is translation. Translation is, for Ricoeur, the "only known remedy for the dispersion and confusion of languages ..." (Ricoeur 2010, 38). Through translation we can proceed laterally and aroristically in our inclusive dialogues. As Gadamer writes, "The multiplicity of languages does not represent an insurmountable barrier ... Every language is teachable. Thus a person is always capable of overcoming all boundaries [represented by language], when that person seeks to reach an understanding with the other person" (Gadamer 2007, 418). Even if we hear an unfamiliar language, we can detect the possibility of acquiring fluency in it for dialogue. Indeed, as Gadamer points out, "one more easily makes oneself understood in the stuttering of a foreign language than when ... each [speaks] his or her own mother tongue" (Gadamer 2007, 418). Translation and learning more languages stand in opposition to some "overhead perspective" that claims to "embrace the totality of the religious field" (Ricoeur 2010, 38). Translation and learning languages oppose, too, the supposed relativism or incommensurability of language communities. As the philosophical theologian of interfaith dialogue Marianne Moyaert clarifies this: "Translation is never just putting one set of ideas and concepts into the language of another; rather, it is the risky enterprise of letting strange ideas interact and change one another. Translation makes meaning[s] move" (Moyaert 2010, 86).

Perhaps some of us wish for something like telepathy instead, some superpower to "read" others' minds without tripping up on language and miscommunication. What this science-fiction fantasy about telepathy reveals is a kind of nihilism (Nietzsche 2008). Not the sci-fi productions in comics where we imagine actual powers of telepathy, but our common deflationary expressions where we sigh and say, "I just wish we had telepathy." Or when in a tyrannical way we desire telepathy to control others. To long for telepathy like this is, as with religious fervor for an apocalypse, an expression of *the desire not to be human* (see Feuerbach 1989, 109–110). The desire not to be human, not to be what we are, is exposed by Nietzsche and others as kind of nihilism. In that sense, it really is a desire not to exist at all. Wishing not to exist often is accompanied by bad faith, a willful ignorance about this wish and denial about it. However, this is an existential contradiction: wanting to *not* exist is literally still a form of existence! In frustration with what we perceive as limitations of language, we wish to experience, understand, and know things in ways very different from our current one. As Kant explains, we wish to "possess a faculty of knowledge totally different from the human one, not only in degree but even in kind and in its [receptivity]—in fact, that we should not be human, but be beings of whom we ourselves could not say whether they are even possible, much less what they would be like" (Kant 2007, 275/B334). When we examine telepathy more technically, we can identify contradictions in the notion, too. In terms of a superpower, it can work as transmitting information and thoughts to others, as receiving information or thoughts that others have, or as manipulating others' minds. In each of these cases, interpretation is still required. How can we "read" another's mind without interpretation? And if "reading" is what happens in telepathy, then are others' thoughts like written language? Can a telepath read someone's mind who speaks a completely different language, as if there is an access without the mediation of language or access to thought independent of any language?

For this chapter on the mediums of interpretation, I want to argue for a few things. I want to emphasize that our understanding is structured linguistically. When people say that "words get in the way," do they know what they are saying? Or, really, do they know—ironically—they are using language to critique what they perceive as a shortcoming of language? Language is the medium in which all interpretation happens. That does not mean that interpretation happens in this or that specific language system, such as Arabic, Thai, or Spanish. Language systems are not technically language yet. They are preparatory for it. But language, living language, is what is happening when we are actually speaking with one another. In other words, language is intrinsically dialogical; it happens in dialogue. I will turn to hermeneutic theories of the work that artworks can do. Artworks can transport and transform us, and this reveals a power to language unlocked by interpretation. This allows us to refine the hermeneutic priority of questioning. Questioning opens us to receive, consider, and even appropriate meanings or complete thoughts.

Interpretation always Happens in Language

Maybe you have heard a friend or loved one say, "Words just cannot express or do justice to my feelings for you." Is this due to how profound and deep their feelings are? Or is this due to their limited vocabulary? If they just knew more words or different languages, perhaps they could express what they feel. I am not stating this to be rude or demeaning to people's deep feelings and experiences. I am trying to shift our attention away from those feelings and experiences to language. When someone says, "words are limited," they are trying to emphasize their profound and deep feelings and experiences. Yet they are making a claim about language, that there is something about language that inhibits rather than facilitates communication and connection about what really matters. As I have elaborated in more detail elsewhere, we often express dissatisfaction with language and interpretation (see Dickman 2016, 256–257; Dickman 2021a, 41–42; Dickman 2022a, 32). We express despair and disappointment when we do not understand some things. The critical anthropologist of religions Talal Asad, for example, examines our feeling horrified by suicide bombings, writing, "Breaking into this paranoid [frenzy] may be the sudden realization that in any death there is nothing to understand—that there's no role for the meaning-making subject. The thought that makes chance deaths more horrible is that they cannot be redeemed by a comforting story" (Asad 2008, 129). Horrifying acts like this seem to challenge all our conventions for making sense of our world and experience. The inability to redeem events through language and interpretation seems to be news, though, as if we expect and even demand to interpret horrifying events but are shocked when we find we cannot. Is the limit of language and interpretation the problem or is our expectation the problem? Is it possible to confuse what is and what is not understandable?

We seem to think language is heterogeneous against reality and what really matters. We believe there is some nonlinguistic reality we must use language to represent accurately, or else what we say is meaningless. As the philosopher of language Ludwig Wittgenstein explains in his early writings, a proposition (complete thought) is a picture, and a true proposition corresponds to factual states of affairs (Wittgenstein 1999, 35). Wittgenstein writes, "Most propositions and questions, that have been written about philosophical [and religious] matters, are not false, but senseless" (Wittgenstein 1999, 45). When we try to say something that does not correspond to facts, in this view, we are speaking nonsense. Most religious philosophies claim there are some realities that essentially exceed the limits of our capacity for linguistic representation. Religious people often protest that their ultimate reality or divine being is beyond concepts and our finite representations (see Edelglass and Garfield 2009, 103). Ultimate realities or beings such as gods like Vishnu or HaShem, celestial bodhisattvas like Avalokiteshvara, and even the Dao, or transcendent ideas such as the Christian trinity, the Buddhist notion of shunyata, and Kant's notion of the Unconditioned, or even horrifying historical evils like the Shoah (or "Holocaust")—all these are said to be essentially outside or beyond language. As Wittgenstein says, "These nonsensical expressions [are] not nonsensical because I [have] not yet found the correct expressions, but their nonsensicality [is] their very essence" (Wittgenstein 1965, 11).

An especially troubling case to illuminate the limits of language is the Shoah. Who has the right to speak or write about the Holocaust—only survivors? A fundamental moral suspicion with regard to discourse about the Holocaust is that it "involves a certain violation of its victims: To speak their experience would run the risk of understanding that experience, with its concurrent possibilities of trivializing or betraying it ... [Speech] inevitably effaces the victim's traumatic experience, and this effacement runs the risk of perpetuating the wrong done to the victim" (Mandel 2001, 222–224). The idea is that the Holocaust exceeds all limits of our abilities to represent it in language. It is so horrible that it is unspeakable. The Jewish theologian Saul Friedlander illustrates this concern in asking, "Why do we feel that Picasso's 'Guernica' forcefully expresses the horror of the death and destruction brought about by the German attack on this peaceful Spanish town, whereas we do not know of any visual expression, nor can we clearly think of any, that would adequately express the utter horror of the extermination of the Jews of Europe?" (Friedlander 2001, 286). Such emphasis on the unspeakability of the Holocaust is reiterated in various ways. Adorno states, "To write poetry after Auschwitz is barbaric" (Adorno 1955, 34). The historian of medieval France Peter Haidu states, "The unspeakability of the Event ... enters into a tradition of the ineffability which attends appearances of the divine [in negative theology]" (Haidu 1992, 284). The Holocaust studies philosopher Berel Lang asks, "Is the enormity of the Holocaust at all capable of literary representation?" (Lang 1988, 2). The Reform rabbi and Jewish philosophical theologian Emil Fackenheim claims it is impossible to understand the Holocaust and that it has no meaning (Fackenheim 1986, 101).

I want to take a different approach to these problems with language's purported limitations. I want to emphasize that I do not intend in any way to demean survivors of trauma with my contribution. My hope, rather, is to reorient ourselves with regard to language, as a kind of therapeutic offering if we can grasp the substance of what I have to say. My proposal, derived from hermeneutic philosophy, is that only language—specifically sentences that answer to questions we actually ask—can be understood. As Gadamer writes, "Being that can be understood is language" (Gadamer 2013, 490; see also Rorty 2004). The word "meaning" is the proper name for the kind of being we understand. We use this word in many ways, as a synonym for a dictionary definition, for an intention to act, for a purpose or significance, or even for an interpretation. However, as noted before, I want us to maintain focus exclusively on sentential sense or complete thoughts grasped in light of questions we ask. This restriction of meaning to complete thoughts should liberate us from the existential angst that accompanies concerns about the limit of language. What is the meaning of life? It has no meaning because "life" is not a sentence. When Fackenheim states that the Shoah has no meaning and when Asad emphasizes that suicide-bombings inhibit our capacity for meaning-making, this is not due to the fact that they are horrifying. The impossibility of understanding them is because they are events, not sentences or answers to questions. This can feel evasive instead of helpful, as if this is just a word-game. I want us to see that the emphasis—or perhaps overemphasis—on the unspeakability of certain events or feelings or ideas can be mere self-congratulatory moralism. As the critical theorist Naomi Mandel explains, rhetorical performance is not ethical practice (Mandel 2001, 206). The real problem is our complicity in these injustices, horrors, or profundities. All of these issue ethical imperatives, such as with the Shoah that we should never forget or trivialize it, and never betray those victims and survivors of it. As Mandel writes, "If we cannot 'know' Auschwitz [a synecdoche for the Shoah], how can we know what not to betray, how not to trivialize, when to remember, why not to forget?" (Mandel 2001, 218).

With a rigorous specification of meaning as the determination of sentential subjects and predicates, we can diagnose these angst-filled questions as making category mistakes. They confuse the order of undergoing experiences with the order of understanding meanings. Experiences or events are not said at all and so are not available for understanding. Only sentences are said. Discourse does not make experience or events directly present as if our minds are transparent to reality without the influence of prejudices—this is what we developed in the previous chapter. When people share a story about an experience they had, do we try to understand those people or what those people *say*? Consider all those times friends have said, "I get you" or "I don't understand you." These are abbreviations for what really happens with understanding. As Gadamer writes, "Where a person is concerned with the other as individuality—e.g., in a therapeutic conversation or the interrogation of a man accused of a crime—this is not really a situation in which [different] people are trying to come to an understanding" (Gadamer 2013, 403). The focus in understanding is on what someone says, not who they are. The point is that while we can empathize with another person, that does not indicate we understand what they are saying. Empathy is like a reflex—when you see someone yawn, it can make you yawn too! We can also understand what someone says without feeling empathetic.

The order of understanding pertains to discursive meanings; the order of experience pertains to events. Events recede, but meanings remain. As Ricoeur writes:

> My experience cannot directly become your experience. An event belonging to one stream of consciousness cannot be transferred as such into another ... Yet, nevertheless, something passes from me to you ... This something is not the experience as experienced, but its meaning. Here is the miracle: The experience as experienced, as lived, remains private, but its sense, its meaning, becomes public. Communication in this way is the overcoming of the radical noncommunicability of the lived experience as lived.
>
> (Ricoeur 1976, 16–19)

Understanding discourse—and even hallucinating the unfurling of images through reading or listening—is not the same as having a direct experience or being immediately present to a referenced event. Experience and events surely are the unsayable limit, but this is just to tell us that the grammar of "meaning" and the grammar of "experience" are distinct. We need to resist, then, asking about the meaning of an experience or the meaning of an event. Instead, more fitting questions concern whether I understand the meaning of what is said with reference to an experience or what is said with reference to the Shoah. If only sentential answers to asked questions can be understood, then our worry about the meanings of life or the Shoah is not a problem of understanding proper, but *a problem of our inflated expectations for understanding*. We try to smear understanding across everything. We demand to understand everything, as if we are entitled to understanding everything. Or we shrug off quests for understanding with indifference, saying, "Some things are a mystery." The point here is that we cannot understand such things because they are not sentences or complete thoughts. We participate in events, undergo experiences, meet others, make something of ourselves, and all these generate in us a drive to speak. However, we understand discourse—no more, no less. Other scholars conceive of "discourse" in far broader terms of social structures or systems, such as the Foucault-inspired approach to language as a social practice. Foucault analyzes discourse within social practices instead of abstracting it from living conditions, as in some linguistics and analytic philosophy. The social practices, however, contain more than just discourse. It is instead that we cultivate and curate, and misrecognize, those dimensions via discourse production and interpretation. I am merely making this explicit when I restrict discourse just to words and sentences.

My restriction of understanding solely to discourse, to words and sentences, liberates us from desperate attempts to understand what literally is not understandable. More importantly, this preserves the underlying moral commitment of the rhetoric of unspeakability. Recall that rhetorical performance ("Words cannot express my feelings for you!") is not enough for moral practice. Nevertheless, we do need to respect others' autonomy to speak for themselves and not efface the traumatic experiences of victims and survivors. My restriction protects people from assimilation, from the reduction of their experiences to mere modifications of my same experience. Empathy can be condescending, such as when people say, "I know exactly how you feel." We do not understand people as if they are mere objects for understanding. People are not complete thoughts. This should not feel disappointing! The trouble is with our expectations or our demands to understand. We should never have expected to understand people or events in the first place. These grammatical distinctions between the order of understanding and the order of events should protect others from naïve assimilation and protect understanding from inflated pretention. I do not understand you but understand what you say.

I want to add one more point here. Many people react to limitations with frustration, as if limitations are always to the detriment of our individual or collective freedom. This feeling stands in tension with what I noted just above that our restriction of understanding liberates us. Yet, for example, without the rules of driving—like speed limits, right-of-way, maintaining traffic operations—people would not be free to get anywhere. Or consider Shariah law with decisions about what is obligatory or forbidden. The five pillars of salat, the Hajj, fasting for Ramadan, zakat, and saying the Shahada or statement of faith are definitive of what it is to be Muslim (see Ayoub 2004). Without these structures, people would not be free to be Muslim. Think of games, too. Without the rules of basketball, for instance, we would not be free to play basketball. There are only six strings on standard guitars, and yet we can imagine nearly an infinite variety of songs. The point here is that restrictions can liberate us as much as they can box us in. Restricting understanding to discourse, to complete thoughts, does not *necessarily* inhibit our freedom.

Let us turn to specify the kind of language at stake in our restriction of understanding.

Dialogue Is the Heart of Language

As above, I want to forge more distinctions to help make gains in clarification and specification. We can communicate in many ways. Language is one among them. However, we need to keep clear about the difference between language systems—such as Spanish, Hebrew, or Tlingit—and discourse. As we noted in the Introduction, there are no words in dictionaries or thesauruses. Lexical entries and grammatical rules are preparatory for discourse but not yet an instance of it. Before the internet, dictionaries and encyclopedias were published as bound books. Let us take Merriam-Webster's dictionary for example. We never read the dictionary to identify the thesis statement or main plot. Can you imagine someone attempting to determine the author's intent with a dictionary? Asking something like, "What is this author trying to say?!?" This is trying to get at the author's explicit intent, the claim or thesis they make or the main plot of a narrative. These have integrative functions. Dictionaries do not. We can ask critical questions about the production of the book, such as about the economic or political interests of a specific dictionary from a specific era. But these are not about the author's intent. Further still, can readers make the text of a dictionary mean whatever they want? Should we let the text speak for itself? These sorts of questions are more or less absurd with regard to dictionaries. This is because dictionaries establish and refine language systems. We make use of these varying systems when we actually speak. They are preparatory for discourse. Discourse, the term, identifies our actual speaking in distinction from language systems. Discourse is temporary, an event that occurs, as Ricoeur writes, "in the succession of events which constitute the diachronic dimension of time ..." (Ricoeur 1976, 3). That is, an instance of discourse happens and then recedes into the past. Language systems, however, are synchronic—existing outside time or at all times along with every instance of discourse. Moreover, a discourse is intended, whereas language systems are anonymous or not intended. We can reify or objectify language systems and study them scientifically. We can make them objects of investigation. This is what a dictionary or a grammar textbook is: the objectified language system. It is something we can investigate. But discourse is that by which we can even conduct investigations. Like consciousness or genuine subjectivity, how can we make into an object the very activity by which we objectify everything else?

If we focus on language systems as paradigmatic or normative for what language really is, our theory of language turns into a theory of signs or names. From this perspective, we think language starts with individual labels or signs. There are two predominant theories of signs originating in ancient Greek philosophy (see Gadamer 2013, 424–428). One promotes a natural relation between the sign and the thing it signifies. Onomatopoeia is a perfect example of this, such as with the words "buzz," "whip," or "crash." This is an attempt to answer how words represent or correspond to things. The other attempt is based on conventions, that the association of signs with things is arbitrary. Since all languages are human inventions, there is no natural relation between words and things. This alternative to the theory focused on natural correspondence purports to explain why there are diverse languages. Each culture has its own conventions for creating and organizing signs. The medieval Buddhist philosophers Dignaga and Dharmakirti, alternatively, developed a third theory of language called "*apoha*" or exclusion (Gillon 2013, 315). In Buddhist cosmology, as noted in the last chapter, all things are defined by emptiness or *shunyata*—there is no thing or object there at which a sign or label points. It is a symptom of our fundamental ignorance to believe there are discretely existing things, and that we create suffering when we try to cling to them. The apoha theory of language is a system of exclusion, where concepts are developed and clarified on their difference from other concepts—not on their accuracy to some mind-independent reality. That is, *words and things do not have any connection!*

When signs are taken as paradigmatic or normative for how language works, complete thoughts become distorted into just bigger or elongated signs. We can learn to manipulate and process signs without understanding their meanings, like a parrot mimicking human speech. Again, we can distinguish semiotics—the study of signs—from semantics—the study of complete thoughts or meanings. The philosopher of rhetoric Michel Meyer calls this the "propositionalist ideology" (Meyer 1995). Propositions, or complete thoughts, are construed as pictures of facts, where true propositions and the facts they picture run parallel to one another. Sentences in different language systems express the "same" proposition. The Spanish sentence "La nieve es blanca," for example, supposedly expresses the same proposition as the German sentence "Der Schnee ist weiß" and the English sentence "The snow is white." Yet what are the questions that these different sentences attempt to answer? The point is that there are many attempts to explain the relation(s) between the world and words, between the world and language systems. Mathematical and logical symbols seduce us into conceiving of language these ways (see Gadamer 2013, 430). When we reduce language to a pile of words or system of signs, "number" becomes the real paradigm for how language is supposed to work. While we can communicate through exchanging signs with one another, discourse involves understanding meanings.

What these positions overlook is taking dialogue as normative for discourse instead of signs. Conversation is the basic unit of language, not the sentence or even the word (see Everett 2017, 68). Living languages are those in use, those we use in dialogue with one another. We can approach dialogue as a practice or game. There are distinctive goals definitive for it, standards of excellence by which we assess actions aimed at achieving those goals, heroes who embody those excellent actions, and rules definitive for the field of action (see Dickman 2021a, 147–153; MacIntyre 1981, 187–191). Like the rules for basketball set us free to play it, and like the mitzvoth laws set us free to be Jewish, so do the rules of dialogue set us free to understand. As the ethicist Alasdair MacIntyre explains, games and practices are "any coherent and complex form of socially established cooperative human activity through which goods internal to that form of activity are realized in the course of trying to achieve those standards of excellence which are appropriate to, and partially definitive of, that form of activity ..." (MacIntyre 1981, 187). Virtuous actions facilitate our effort reach toward standards of excellence and goods internal to the activity. Vicious actions inhibit this. When we learn these skills and hone our effort, we can transfer these skills to further activities.

I think the goal of dialogue can be pinpointed with Gadamer as "being at one on a subject matter" (Gadamer 2013, 403). We can also refer to this as a fusion of horizons, where two people come together in discussion, and through this exchange of questions and answers each person's perspective is transformed. This is the unique thing we can achieve only through dialogue and nowhere else. Maybe some people think that the goal of dialogue is to acquire information. But we can do this with an encyclopedia. We do not need dialogue for that. In a game, we are "at one" when we achieve a concentrated flow state with one another. Gadamer describes this by saying that games fill us with their dynamic spirit, which surpasses us as isolated individuals trying to control things (Gadamer 2013, 112). Games take us over. People sometimes even describe it as "losing myself" in the game. Good dialogues work this way, too. It is difficult to try to control or conduct a conversation like this. No one sits us down and says, "Okay, let's start a good dialogue right now!" For me, I always look back with surprise for having had a good dialogue.

The freedom that comes through the rules of dialogue also comes with a kind of purposelessness. This is true of all play, really (see Gadamer 2013, 107). What is the point of playing music? Theater? Sports? Many people try to provide scientific explanations for them, such as listening to Mozart helps children's brains develop. Do we really need this to justify enjoying music? Is that even the point of music? Do we need scientific research to prove that *salat* five times a day is healthy for our lower backs? Moreover, good dialogues seem full of tangents and varieties of topics—some related and some not. Sometimes a conversation starts off about one topic, but then shifts entirely to another without return to the first one that set off the discussion. It is as if the aim of dialogue is truly the back-and-forth play of these dynamics. If we try to steer or control the dialogue, we might try to insist on our point of view, distorting the dialogue into a mere debate. As Gadamer writes:

> [I]t belongs to every true [dialogue] that each person opens himself to the other, truly accepts his point of view as valid and transposes himself into the other to such an extent that he understands not the particular individual but *what he says*. What is to be grasped is the substantive rightness of his opinion, so that we can be at one with each other on the subject [matter].
>
> (Gadamer 2013, 403; my emphasis)

Remember, it is not about empathy but about understanding. Just as we cannot objectify ourselves to ourselves with complete access, we cannot objectify another person. They are contributors to our dialogue as much as we are. It is like the game seesaw. When we think about the point of seesaw, is it just for exercise? Is there a way to win, where one person does so, and the other person loses? To me, seesaw is a team exercise to bring about the uninhibited back and forth movement, where we lose ourselves in making this movement present. That is the freedom of play, following the rules. Sometimes, spoilsports will ruin the play, perhaps by jumping off and letting their partner crash to the ground like a prank. The spoilsport acts as if they are free, free from the rules of the game. In reality, we only reach that beautiful kind of recreational freedom within the structure set by the rules. When we get to that back-and-forth movement, though, there is nothing like it!

The philologist Max Müller is famous for having said about diverse languages, "He who knows only one, knows none" (Müller 1873, 16). This seems connected with language systems, where we need fluency in multiple language systems. In a way, this is true. How can we become self-conscious of our language *as a language* if we do not have a contrast for it with another language? Monolingual people—or, rather, people who are naïve about the language they speak—experience their language as a singular transparent access to the real world (see Rothman 2008). It is as if language directly represents reality, as if a person has no bias or prejudice. When we build up fluency in an additional language system or language-game, we start to recognize both limitations and subtleties that occur in only one language or the other—or we even find ways to combine fluencies into one improvisational flow. More importantly, however, our goal is to reach one another in dialogue. When we listen to another person, we might be pulled up short in our understanding with the way they speak with their idiosyncratic use of words. That is, just because we supposedly speak the same language—as in we both use the same language system—that does not entail that we use the words in the same way. Knowing more than one language also means that we can listen to another person and understand what they have to say without forcing what they say into our preferred terms or worldview. In other words, Müller's point is just as much about the need to listen to others in dialogue as it is about language systems. We should not focus on signs or propositions in our development of language as primarily dialogical. Instead, let us turn to the relation between art and predication.

Language Is an Artwork Rather than a Collection of Labels on Things

Dialogue, as the heart of language, consists of a dialectic of questions and sentences that answer to those questions (Dickman 2021a, 161–181). As Ricoeur states, it is in sentences that language "is formed and takes shape," where language really begins (Ricoeur 2003, 79). What makes sentences distinctive from signs, what makes complete thoughts not mere propositions, is that they have predicates (see Ricoeur 1976, 10). Predicates help us resist reduction of discourse to mere representative propositions or mere names. As Ricoeur writes, "Although naming is an important 'language game,' the overestimation of the word and even fascination with words, pushed to the point of superstition, reverence, or terror, are due perhaps to a basic illusion ... that the naming game is the paradigm of all language games" (Ricoeur 2003, 150). In this approach to language, as we noted, propositions are representations that run parallel to the world. Predicates are reduced to mere attributes to sentential subjects. This is a superficial view of language, a stagnancy in thinking. Instead of an ever-renewing and ever-blossoming dialogue, thinking bottoms out in (in)accurate representation. We distort predicates when we conceive of language in this way.

Predicates, however, illuminate the predicament of sentential subjects, their relevant context (see Kant 2007, 106–107; Dickman 2021a, 17–19). Predicates supersede subjects. They do not "represent" them. Instead, they *present* them. They embody radiant aspectival presences of subject matters in understanding, where an aspect of truth emerges through dialogue in questions and responses. Consider this sentence, "This sunset is beautiful!" It is not that there is this metaphysically discrete entity we call a "sunset." We know the Sun does not rotate around Earth. That is, sunsets do not actually exist. Therefore, the predicate "is beautiful" cannot be a mere attribute of an existent thing, some "fact" that exists in a real world. Recall in phenomenology, though, that we bracket out our natural or scientific perspective. While we know that sunsets do not exist, we are conscious of our experience *as* looking at a sunset. And this is not just any sunset, but a beautiful one. The predicate makes our reality present to our consciousness, to our understanding. As Beauvoir explains, consciousness is about disclosing being or reality—through understanding, we make the world present (Beauvoir 2015, 11). Language, when it works, has its being in its revealing like a windshield allowing the road to be present. It is not that we perceive a sunset, and then place it in the category of "beautiful." It is that the sunset is made present to us in its radiant beauty. Predicates hook subjects into fields of intelligibility, and this way we can understand complete thoughts that address our questions. We can illuminate this with more examples. What direction are you facing? Is it forward, or North, or toward Mecca? Each of these three options are different calculi for orientation. Egocentric directions include forward, backward, left, and right. Cardinal directions overlay our orientation in accord with the poles of the planet. The Qibla compass helps us know what direction to face when praying *salat*. That is, each orientation system is a field of intelligibility. A statement such as, "This direction is toward Mecca" hooks the subject into a field of intelligibility, orienting us within a Muslim world of significance.

Upward metaphors come to mind for conceiving of how predication works. Rather than running parallel to the world like representation, hooking into fields of intelligibility moves our understanding perpendicularly to the world. When predicates supersede subjects, they "lift" subjects into a "higher order." Predication is, as Ricoeur writes, "nothing other than *the elevation of part of our life into the logos of discourse*. There the solitude of life is for a moment, anyway, illuminated by the common light of discourse" (Ricoeur 1976, 19; my emphasis). Predicates "raise" subjects into the "light" of understanding. In this approach, language is not a redundant layer but an animation of the world where chaos transforms into order and intelligibility. Recall that it is through order, through rules, that we realize freedom. Without constitutive rules governing a field of activity, we cannot be free to create or to actualize ourselves. In other words, these upward metaphors correlate to increased freedom of the mind. (If you read the Preface, I want readers to recall the discussion of writing and freedom of mind.)

The German Idealist philosopher Georg Wilhelm Friedrich Hegel explains this in his theory of fine art. For Hegel, human created art is more beautiful than mere natural sights (Hegel 1997, 23–24). Art is higher because it expresses our freedom. This is not in the sense of mere creativity or spontaneity. It is the freedom to externalize our mind or spirit (Hegel 1997, 29). A sunset—or, rather, an earth-spin—is a matter of necessity and regularity. It still might be beautiful, but it is not free. Only our spirits externalize truths when we make a statement with our artworks. By virtue of externalization, though, we can come back to ourselves. Like a diary, we can see ourselves outside ourselves, and thus achieve a self-understanding. We realize ourselves in our work; we make ourselves actual. As Hegel writes:

> Man is realized for himself by practical activity, inasmuch as he has the impulse, in the medium which is directly given to him, to produce himself, and therein at the same time to recognize himself. This purpose he achieves by the modification of external things upon which he impresses the seal of his inner being, and then finds repeated in them his own characteristics. Man does this in order as a free subject to strip the outer world of its stubborn foreignness, and to enjoy in the shape and fashion of things a mere external reality of himself.
> (Hegel 1997, 58)

We make something of ourselves through our work and labor. This is one fundamental way that neoliberal capitalism dehumanizes us—in being separated as mere wageworkers from the products of our labor so that capitalists might profit from those products, we literally are separated from ourselves. We are alienated from ourselves. Ideally, we achieve self-integration, an expansion of ourselves. We grow by broadening our horizons in appropriating back to ourselves that which we have externalized in art. As Hegel illustrates this, "Even the child's first impulse involves the practical modification of external things. A boy throws stones in the river, and then stands admiring the circles that trace themselves on the water, as an effect in which he attains the sight of something that is his own doing" (Hegel 1997, 58). *By perceiving ourselves outside ourselves, by alienating or othering ourselves from ourselves, we create space for growth and greater self-understanding.*

Artworks are material and concrete embodiments of the human spirit or consciousness, in its attempt at self-realization. They are the exteriorization of consciousness, so that we can understand ourselves in our radical otherness. As Mbembe describes this:

> The primary function of the work of art has never been to represent, illustrate, or narrate reality. It has always been in its nature simultaneously to confuse and mimic original forms and appearances ... In most Black aesthetic traditions, art was produced only through the work of conjuring, in the space where the optic and tactile functions, along with the world of the senses, were united in a single movement aimed at revealing the double of the world. In this way the time of a work of art is the moment when daily life is liberated from accepted rules and is devoid of both obstacles and guilt.
>
> (Mbembe 2017, 173)

However, this is a struggle, where meaningful worlds of interrelated webs of significance burst out of earthy materiality. At the same time, the earth swallows these worlds (see Heidegger 2001, 47–48). The earth swallows all remnants of past life, as archeologists know. What we make breaks down. Like a car that rusts, the elements disintegrate what we make. Or sediment collects and covers it over. Yet out of the elements, we build worlds, interconnected webs of significance. I always think of autostereograms (or perhaps better known by the trademarked name "Magic Eye") as a model or analogy for this phenomenon (see the Appendix). In an autostereogram, there is an image with a repeating pattern (the elements of the earth), but if you look at it just right, a three-dimensional object emerges (the world of significance). The science is that we can manipulate our two eyes, where we adjust them to fold the image into itself to create sensations of depth with a background and a foreground. It is the same technology used by the British military to detect Nazi assets during World War II. Where does this virtual object exist? Not in the elements of the image. It is in our understanding, our capacity to grasp the truth. Moreover, this truth is objective—we can say things that are true or false about what we perceive as the three-dimensional object. In the Appendix, for instance, there is one gorilla and two bananas. If someone said there are eight gorillas and one banana, they would be incorrect. Even more, the kind of truth revealed is alethic or "unconcealment" (see Hegel 1997, 87; Heidegger 2001, 49). Out of the environment of elements, truth happens. Art makes truth happen.

This is how predicates work, too. As Ricoeur writes, "The world is the ensemble of [subjects] opened up by every kind of text, descriptive or poetic, that I have read, understood, and loved. And to understand a text is to interpolate among the predicates of our situation all the significations that make a *Welt* out of our *Umwelt*" (Ricoeur 1976, 37). That is, these interpolated or interconnected predicates transform our mere environment (*Umwelt*) into a meaningful world (*Welt*). Predicates reveal the truth of the subject. Predicates have their being in their revealing the essence or gravy of a subject. It is like a miniature version of the comparative mythologist Joseph Campbell's notion of the hero's journey. Just like the hero leaves home, goes through trials and tribulations, and returns home changed, so too are subjects lifted into the intelligibility of the predicate to return to itself changed. What else is a sentence but an abbreviated narrative or hero's journey? However, just like all artistic work, predicative work to produce and understand complete thoughts is imperiled by being buried beneath mere signs. That is, a sentence perceived is not a complete thought understood (Dickman 2021a, 28). Rather than facilitating understanding, words can inhibit it. It is like listening to a speech and believing that the speaker's voice sounded nice rather than grasping the content of the person's speech. Or it is like when White people "tone police" objections by Black people to White people's behaviors and statements in an explicit attempt to maintain and advance respectability politics.

The rules for discourse, including both grammatical and logical rules, set thinking and reasoning free. When someone writes an ungrammatical sentence, the materiality of the sentence stands out—like the glass of the windshield. Think of all the corrections our primary school teachers marked us down for: split infinitive, missing a subject, new paragraph needed, dangling modifier, run-on sentence, etc. We do not need to reinvent the wheel every time we speak or write or sign. Through the accumulation of usage, we become more experienced with what works and what does not work to communicate. Yes, so in a sense, sometimes words do get in the way! It is when they stop functioning as words and dissolve into mere signs or representations. With the varieties of languages and language-games we know that these rules can shift and adjust, but we are never without some rules governing the fields of possible discourse. Similarly, logical laws determine valid and invalid argument forms, what inferences we can make and rely on with certainty or probability. These rules set thinking, reasoning, and understanding free. Without them—as with other constitutive rules like those for driving or basketball or Buddhist practice—we would not be free to do any of them. On the basic level, predication hooks us into these higher order freedoms of our minds made possible in grammars and logics. One logic in particular, the one that transforms sentences perceived into meanings understood, is the logic of question and answer.

Questioning Gives Shape to the Opening of Our Understanding

I argued in Chapter 1 on the predicaments of interpretation that questioning has hermeneutic priority, taking precedence over other options such as the writer's intent or a reader's caprice when determining what a text can mean. I want to spend more time here elaborating on how questioning opens us up to receive meanings, how questioning transforms language perceived into complete thoughts understood.

One entry point that helps me conceive of this is the phenomenologist Maurice Merleau-Ponty's approach to our embodiment. Merleau-Ponty attempts to rethink Husserl's account of intentionality and consciousness outside of Cartesian terms, where consciousness is purportedly something only minds do or have (see Merleau-Ponty 2002). According to Merleau-Ponty, our body—rather than our conscious mind—is the locus of synthesis or unity (Merleau-Ponty 2002, 173). It is not that I have a body, but that I am my body. Moreover, it is not that we have a concept or category of a unified body and then apply it to severed parts to make it one body. Instead, the integrity of our body is like a musical chord, an already unified whole where the parts are derivative rather than primary. The body we are is also assimilative in that technologies become prosthetic enhancements, such as a walking cane or glasses and contact lenses. Once bodily incorporated, these are no longer objects perceived but faculties of our ability to perceive (Merleau-Ponty 2002, 176). Moreover, our bodies are dehiscent—split in two as simultaneously feeling and felt, like when we touch our own hands (Merleau-Ponty 1968, 123). It is misleading to picture this split in the medical terms of an open wound, as if we are torn open. For Merleau-Ponty, our bodily dehiscence is our fundamental openness to the world. However, our natural attitude construes perception and intentionality as conduits that transport representations from "external" things to our minds, like the effluvia model of sensation popular in ancient Roman philosophy and science. Instead of pipelines for impressions, we envelop things within our bodily dehiscence or folds. As Merleau-Ponty points out, this why we say we experience things "*in* the flesh," not *through* the flesh (Merleau-Ponty 2002, 373). Take hearing, for example. It is not merely three hundred and sixty degrees around us, but above and below and within us. It is not a mere pipeline from the sound's source to our mind. Instead, we dehiscently envelop space all around noises (Denny and McFadzean 2011, 183–200). For Merleau-Ponty, this shows embodiment precedes abstract space, as if there is space and then our body is put into this abstract container (Merleau-Ponty 2002, 171; see also Lee 2014, 273). The spatiality of embodiment is more fundamental than "objective space" (see Dickman 2021c). By giving ourselves to ourselves via embodied dehiscence, we generate a network of potential or in other words a conscious "I can."

Just as objects are bodily enveloped, our understanding envelops meanings. Questioning is our opening to meanings and complete thoughts. As Irigaray explains, we should not abstract questioning from the "I can" of embodiment, "from its carnal taking root" (Irigaray 2002, 74). With touch, we can grasp things in the folds of our flesh. Similarly with questioning, we enfold meanings in the flesh of our understanding or the sulci and gyri of our brains. Questioning makes the dehiscence of understanding articulate. It does so because, as Gadamer writes, "all suspension of judgments [i.e. complete thoughts] and hence, a fortiori, of prejudices, has the logical structure of a question" (Gadamer 2013, 310). Questioning maintains a distance from our prejudices, from complete thoughts suggested as answers, while simultaneously holding our understanding open to them as answers we can own via appropriation. Through questioning, we open ourselves to listen to what others say to us and put assumed complete thoughts at risk of criticism and testing. Written, signed, and spoken interrogative sentences embody our opening to meanings. This opening to meanings is where understanding "touches" itself. In this way, sentences perceived are transformed into meanings understood. It is how we ingest, digest, and ruminate on meanings.

Genuine questions do not *say* something, though. Only assertions—explicit or implicit—say something. The propositionalist ideology results from forgetting or neglect of the fact that complete thoughts answer to questions we actually ask (see Dickman 2021a, 60–61). Answers disintegrate into contextless propositions. As the phenomenologist Johannes Daubert emphasizes, questioning does not objectify, does not itself say something about sentential subjects (Schuhmann and Smith 1987, 356; Bruin 2001, 17). Questions do not say something, sentences do and these transform into graspable meanings inasmuch as they answer to questions. This is what allows us to consider meanings or complete thoughts without appropriating them as our own. Recall that when we consider questions, we cannot help but to ask them. This is not so for answers. We can consider them without owning them. Shared questions are what open us to listen to others, what others have to say to us. By listening actively with questions, we can consider what others have to say to us. Without the questions, their statements are lost on us. Their statements have no context or motivation. We cannot relate to what they say.

When we focus on discourse with precision like this, we can narrow and specify a limited number of options and orientations for questioning within discourse. I have addressed these in thorough detail elsewhere, but I will provide them here in summary fashion for clarification (see Dickman 2021a). In the domain of thinking and understanding complete thoughts, questioning coalesces around four poles: the pole of the sentential subject, the pole of the predicate, the pole of the copula, and the pole of questioning itself. There are *subject-centered questions*, the kinds that ask for a subject to be specified like an algebraic variable. Here is an example: What is for dinner? The answer will include the selection of a subject, such as "Pizza is for dinner." Additionally, many questions focus on an indeterminacy within predication, what predicate properly situates a subject. Consider this example: Where is the library? In the question, the sentential subject ("the library") is explicit, but the disclosive predicate is not determined yet. The library might be in a number of places such as "On the corner of 12th and Main" or "Near the Chamber of Commerce," each of which is a unique predicate or predicament. These are what I call *predicament-centered questions* (Dickman 2021a, 45–49). The focus of these questions is on what predicament the subject is in. *Copula-centered questions* attend to whether or not a predicate is properly disclosive of a subject, such as, "People say that 'time is money,' but is it really?" The "is" is the focus of these sorts of questions. And, finally, *question-centered questioning* focuses on the nature or quality of the questioning itself. When asking "Are there more wheels or doors in existence?" we can wonder whether this is asked as a closed question seeking a final solution or whether this is an open-ended question where we can reflect on the nature of wheels, doors, and existence itself.

On the secondary level of understanding, or what properly is called reasoning, we coordinate multiple complete thoughts into logical order. Here there are questions focused on premises, conclusions, inferences, and even rationality itself (Dickman 2021a, 117–122). With *conclusion-centered questioning*, for instance, we have an explicit premise or set of premises and wonder what we can infer from it, what we can conclude from it. Consider this example: "All human beings are mortal, and Socrates is a human being. And so?" It asks for a conclusion. In *premise-centered questions*, we have an explicit conclusion, but seek the premise or multiple options of premises that support the conclusion. Perhaps someone says, "Why should I get a vaccine booster?" The conclusion "You should get a vaccine booster" is supported by one or more premises, such as boosters usually reduce the severity of the effects of the virus. When we ask *inference-centered questions*, we look into the argument form, such as whether the argument is deductive or abductive, and the validity or strength of the form in use. We get reflexive, too, when we undertake *rationality-centered questioning*, such as when we ask whether Western logics like predicate logic can handle the seeming contradictory arguments of Buddhist philosophers like Nagarjuna.

On the third level of understanding, or what properly is called dialogue, we coordinate different arguments or reasonings (Dickman 2021a, 191–194). Here questions focus on theses, antitheses, syntheses, or even dialogue itself. An *antithesis-centered question* focuses on a negative or critical moment in a broader ongoing dialogue, such as when someone throws their hands up and asks, "What is the point of getting an education anyway?" These sorts of questions emerge in light of conversations or cultural traditions that are already underway. It is a sign that we are starting to wake up, and call into question standard ways of doing things. These can turn into deflationary conversation stoppers if we are not careful with them. Alternatively, *thesis-centered questions* are a kind of reminder, where we might ask mid-discussion, "What were we talking about, again?" On a broader level though, these are reconstructive questions, because we can only really get back to some initiating topic after a dialogue is well underway. Dialogues are improvisational, and we find ourselves already in them mid-stream. Another instance of questioning at this level is what I call *synthesis-centered questioning*. Here is an example: In listening to someone else speak in a conversation, we might ask, "Where are they going with this?" When asked disingenuously, this can also be a conversation-stopper. But when asked sincerely, we try to anticipate and add applications to what has been said up to this point. The summit of all levels of questioning are *dialectic-centered questions* or dialogue-centered questions. In a way, the majority of this text on interpretation concerns these sorts of questions, like, "What is the nature and purpose of dialogue itself?" Or, "Can dialogues ever be completed?" These resist any "final solution."

With my specification of all the different coalescing poles for questioning, I want to clarify that there really are only twelve total question kinds when it comes to comprehending discourse. We can ask about complete thoughts, the logical relation of them with one another, and our broad conversations. That is it. My point is that there are a limited set of orientations for questioning, but this actually sets us free rather than restricts us. It may seem like all our questions seek information and that this is an essential element of genuine questions, but this is not so. The phenomenologist Emmanuel Levinas criticizes this, insisting that questioning "cannot be reduced to intentionality, or that *it rests, properly speaking, on an intentionality that fails*" (Levinas 1998, 71; my emphasis). If we just need information, then we do not need to use questions to acquire it. We can turn to search engines or encyclopedias for the information. Questioning, though, does not have to aim at some self-cancelling fulfillment as "knowledge." As Levinas writes,

"Must we not admit, on the contrary, that the request and the prayer that cannot be dissimulated in [questioning] attest to *a relation to the other person* ...? A relation delineated in the question, not just as any modality, but as in its originary one" (Levinas 1988, 72). Questioning embodies relationship with others before it can be instrumentalized as a mere tool to acquire information. That is, questions are more about relationships than about getting answers! Recall our discussion of transcendental intersubjectivity as embodied in dialogue. As an individual, I might have an anxious need for information, like when I am late and ask, "What time is it?" Shared questioning, alternatively, is cooperative, an embodied intermingling that refuses domination in our dehiscent openness to a surplus of meanings (see Lee 2014, 235–236). When we are merely looking for *the* final solution, we close off dialogical possibilities prematurely. In genuine questioning, we do not know ahead of time where we will end up, or even if there will be a "final" answer. As Socrates pictures this, we must follow the discourse wherever it, like the wind, blows (Plato 1991, 394d).

My restriction of questioning and understanding to discourse might feel to some readers like I have atrophied it. Again, to most of us, it seems like everything—not just language—can be understood. Not just that it can be understood, but that everything *should* be understood. We cannot smear understanding across everything, though. Only sentences, only complete thoughts as answers to questions, can be understood. What is the meaning of life? The problem is not that "life" is complex, but that "life" is not a complete thought. As Wittgenstein illustrates, "How do I recognize that this colour is red?—One answer would be: 'I have learnt English'" (Wittgenstein 2009, §381). Grammatical therapy has the power to liberate us from distorting understanding away from discourse to things themselves. Consider another example, such as when someone says, "You will never understand my experience!" It seems like this is a profound statement about the radically private character of experience. That is, it seems like this is a metaphysical claim about the essence of experience. With our restriction of understanding to discourse, though, this does not tell us something about experience. It is, rather, axiomatic about the rules of language, what can and cannot be talked about if the concept "experience" is discussed. For another example, consider the sentence, "Everything just increased by ten times its size." On the surface, this seems to make a paradoxical metaphysical claim about the nature of sizes. Like Wittgenstein, our therapeutic solution is that "everything" cannot work as a subject of a sentence. Sentential subjects specify particular things from out of the backdrop horizon of everything else. Thus, the word "everything" does not do the work that a sentential subject is supposed to do. What I—following Wittgenstein—am trying to point out is that this metaphysical temptation can be resisted by attending more closely to discourse itself.

In this chapter, I have argued that interpretation happens in language, specifically in the mode of dialogue. I have also emphasized that language in its predicative function is disclosive or revelatory like a works of art. And I have isolated how questioning operates in our capacities to connect with other people over meanings we envelop with our understanding. Let us turn to examine ways these play out in writing, transitioning to written texts as the proper objects of interpretation.

Chapter 4

The Objects of Interpretation

We are finally prepared to develop a theory of texts, the objects of interpretation. Notice that we have spent our time so far primarily focused on interpreters and dialogue. These are preparatory for isolating the exceptional phenomenon of written texts.

In this chapter on the objects of interpretation, I want to argue for a few things. I want to revisit the distinction between texts and books. Whereas earlier I clarified *that* texts and books are different, here I want to specify *how* texts are different from books. Building on this difference, I want to examine how written work radically changes discourse, and opens us to a broader horizon of understanding. I will develop four layers of questioning in the reading process by which we enable our comprehension of texts. These different layers can be specified with regard to what we should do with lines of text. I also develop a notion of "classic" texts as paradigmatic for interpretation. It is not that we need to preserve some loyalty to a (Eurocentric) canon of inherited literature, but that classics have the capacity to speak to us across cultures and eras.

Objects of Interpretation Are Texts, Not Books

Just as sentences perceived are not necessarily complete thoughts understood, books we glance over are not necessarily texts we understand. Surely—like all readers—you have experienced "reading" a page in a book, but at the end of the page you think to yourself, "What did I just read?" Yes, in many cases, this may just be a matter of zoning out and losing concentration. I am trying to focus on those occasions where we have decided to read a challenging book, like a work of philosophy or experimental poetry. In these instances, our lack of comprehension is not due to some lack of attention. We know the language and we understand each word in isolation from the others, but when we try to put it all together we do not have a grasp on a specific concept or point being made on the page. To transform a sentence perceived into a complete thought or meaning understood, we need to ask the question to which it responds. Just so with books: we need to ask the questions to which it responds to transform it from a book perceived into a text understood. As we noted before, books are artifacts we can take off and put back on a shelf. Texts, though, are semantic fields that emerge solely in the process of interpretation or the reading process.

In this way, interpretation of written texts in reading has structural parallels to musical performance. As Gadamer writes, "No one believes that reading music is the same as listening to [or performing] it" (Gadamer 2013, 147). That is, there is a difference between the score and the song. The score is an artifact, sitting there inert. The song is a dynamic structure, produced by a performer and enjoyed (or critically appreciated) by an audience. The key, for now, is that performers want to get the song right, just as a cover song sometimes captures the heart of a tune even better than an original version (see Gadamer 2013, xxviii). We can also illustrate this by returning to autostereogram images, where the distorted repeated pattern perceived is the book and the three-dimensional object is the text (see the Appendix). We can say things that are true or false about the repeated pattern, but we can also say things that are true or false about the three-dimensional emergent object. We can also illustrate this though popup books—there is the mere cardboard, and then there is the three-dimensional landscape that emerges through unfolding the cardboard. Children do this in play, too, where they dress up in a costume and want to be treated as the character and become upset if you address them directly instead of the character into whom they have transformed. Like all of these, a book transforms into the dynamic structure of a text (Gadamer 2013, 115–118).

My differentiation between books and texts runs counter to others' approaches, such as Derrida's theory and the evangelical Christian theologian Kevin J. Vanhoozer's attempt at critique of Derrida's theory (see Derrida 1997; Vanhoozer 1998). Both Derrida and Vanhoozer agree that books are as much semantic fields as texts are, and they both agree that while books are closed semantic fields, texts are open-ended semantic fields. Derrida uplifts texts, however; Vanhoozer attempts to retrieve books. As Derrida writes:

> The idea of the book is the idea of a totality, finite or infinite, of the signifier; this totality of the signifier cannot be a totality, unless a totality constituted by the signified preexists it, supervises its inscriptions and its signs, and is independent of it in its ideality ... It is the encyclopedic protection of theology and of logocentrism against the disruption of writing, against its aphoristic energy, and ... against difference in general. If I distinguish the text from the book, I shall say that the destruction of the book ... denudes the surface of the text.
> (Derrida 1997, 18)

An implication here is that books are complete, a complete creation of a stable and central intending writer or creator—ultimately some god behind the book. Books, in other words, signify or refer to their writers. Writing, or text, challenges this stability of centered intentions and transparency of books to some metaphysical reality. Whereas books have a "correct" interpretation, texts are open to a plurality of interpretations or at least allow freedom to grasp varying significances for readers with regard to their communities (see Vanhoozer 1998, 259). Both Derrida and Vanhoozer focus on what we are calling "texts" even though they both use the word "book" to signify a special kind of text. Recall that for us texts are interpretable—whether or not there is one "correct" interpretation. Books, in my stipulation, are not interpretable. They are sheer physical artifacts. This matters because collaborators with Vanhoozer, such as Wolterstorff, use this distinction to dismiss the kind of hermeneutic I am developing here. Wolterstorff writes, "An orthodoxy of twentieth-century theory of interpretation, both continental and Anglo-American, has been that interpretation is an action or set of actions performed upon an artifact, the paradigmatic species of such an artifact being a text. My view is that interpretation at bottom is not things done to an artifact but engagement with a person ..." (Wolterstorff 2006, 36). As I explained in Chapter 1 on the predicaments of interpretation, we need a conception of texts distinct from writers' intentions, yet there is still a voice of the text itself, an "author" *who is a function of the text*. We do engage with this person!

How do texts emerge from books, though? It starts with sentences—or what is on the lines. Recall the etymological connection between text and weaving. The sentences of a book are lines of writing or Braille. When we see or feel lines of a book, they can be right justified or merely left-aligned lines. They might be single-spaced or double-spaced. Can we have double-spaced complete thoughts, though? This is an absurd question. It is not the sentences, but the complete thoughts that are interwoven to create a semantic fabric. Complete thoughts thread together, not sentences. One strange thing is that "fabrication" has come to mean deception or a fake tale. Yet it also means to produce something. How is reading a book productive? Combining a subject and a predicate—via a copula—produces a new being, a meaning or complete thought. Meanings are greater than the sums of their parts. They are of a higher, that is, *freer*, order. Combing multiple complete thoughts, though, does not generate a being of an additional new order. As Ricoeur writes, "There is no unit of a higher order that could provide a generic class for [complete thoughts] conceived as a species. It is possible to connect [complete thoughts] according to an order of concatenation, but not to integrate them" (Ricoeur 1976, 10). That is, no new mode of being emerges through connecting complete thoughts. Concatenation is the linking together of complete thoughts in a series. It is not their synthesis into an even higher (aka freer) mode of being. However, we do observe sedimentation and innovation in patterns of series or genres, such as argumentative essays, confessional poetry, math textbooks, romantic comedies, and more. Usually in discussions of literature, people use "genre" in a classificatory way, for taxonomic labelling useful for bookstores and libraries. Genres are really modes of discourse, though, not mere labels for orienting ourselves in vast seas of books. The etymology of the word "genre" relates to "generate," where genres are generative or productive. It makes sense to call art or literature "works," in the work they do to produce meaningful worlds. Composed whole texts, not mere bound books, present a fabric or texture and, as Ricoeur writes, "calls for an interpretation of its inner organization. Understanding a text is always something more than the summation of its partial meanings; the text as a whole has to be considered as a hierarchy of topics" (Ricoeur 1974, 74). When we identify the thesis statement or the plot, we align the other complete thoughts under it. It is not merely that writers can use genres as guidelines for arranging the series of their complete thoughts; readers too can use genres to guide their interpretation of the series of complete thoughts. Once generated, a semantic embroidery emerges in the field of understanding—like a popup book or three-dimensional entity out of an autostereogram image (see the Appendix).

What emerges is not only a meaningful world but also a speaker—who is an element of the text—and this speaker says something to readers. Texts speak. Books do not. This speaker cannot be identical with the writer, and this is especially apparent in cases where the writer is dead. Barthes writes, "The one who speaks (in the narrative) is not the one who writes (in real life) and the one who writes is not the one who is" (Barthes 1975, 261). We need to resist the temptation to look behind the book for some historical person or metaphysical entity like a god. This voice, Ricoeur writes, "...is an instance of the text ..." (Ricoeur 1995, 191; see also Foucault 1998). This speaker is not behind the book, but in front of the text. Authors are, Barthes writes, "paper beings" (Barthes 1975, 261). I prefer to say they are semantic beings, in light of Ricoeur's concept of semantic autonomy (Ricoeur 1976, 30). As noted, the autonomy is in this persona or ability of the text to speak for itself. This is not quite accurate, though. This speaker is dependent on readers to active its voice. Readers must make texts speak (see Gadamer 2013, 382; Barthes 1975, 261). As Gadamer writes, "It is universally true of texts that only in the process of understanding them is the dead trace of meaning transformed back into living meaning" (Gadamer 2013, 163). However, when someone is forced to speak in face-to-face conversation, this is dehumanizing—perhaps just as dehumanizing as silencing another's voice. The text's voice speaks only in actual reading of the text. Of course, books do not literally speak. What happens, rather, can be clarified by noting what happens when we read aloud. Like recitation, reading aloud is for an audience of listeners. Reading is something we do for someone else. To do this well, we need to bring the words and sentences into harmonious resonance with the complete thoughts or meanings being said (see Gadamer 1989, 47). Think about how parents or guardians sound out voices of characters in children's stories, such as sounding out different animals in different registers to mimic their noises. A teacher can tell by the sound and rhythm of students reading aloud to the class whether the reading student really understands what is written. In this way, readers suture or graft their reading voice to the script or "code" given by the text (Barthes 1975, 265; Ricoeur 1986, 130–131). This is precisely the goal of contestants' performances in Quranic recitation competitions (see Sells 2007, 1). When we read to ourselves silently, we internalize this process and cacophony of sutured or grafted voices. When we read, we read *to* ourselves. The book binds a score through which a reader coordinates a dialogue between two subjectivities—the reader as the one read to, and the reader as the one reading. In reading to oneself, there is both the reader sutured or grafted to the voice of the text who says something and the reader as the receiver to whom this something is said (Dickman 2022a, 48).

It is one thing to say that texts speak. I want to add that this voice of the text listens, too. Many people say this or that song "speaks" to them. What about listening? Can a song "get" you? In other words, can texts listen? Does this even make sense?! Irigaray writes, "In order to talk to the other, to listen to the other, to hold a dialogue between us, we have to again find an artistic, musical, touchful way of speaking or saying and *of listening able to be perceived in a written text*, then not reduced to a simple assistance for remembering meaning or to some code to be respected" (Irigaray 2002, xx; my emphasis). Texts are not mere repositories for memories. They are conversation partners. One way we can detect a text listening to readers is when the text asks questions, specifically genuine questions (see Dickman 2022a). Before we turn to more discrete functions of questions in interpretation, I want to bring out another thread about written works to weave together with what we have covered so far.

Writing Explodes the Given Environment and Refigures the World

Interpreting written works has the power to transform us, to broaden the horizons of our lifeworld in three ways. It transforms the relationship between speaker and listener, it drastically alters the nature of reference, and it creates a radical alienation that *might* be overcome with a proper hermeneutic framework. As we just noted, reading texts cannot be structurally parallel to partners in face-to-face dialogue. Writer and reader in the act of reading do not correlate to speaker and listener in conversation. The reader is absent from the activity of writing, and the writer—as we noted—is absent from the activity of reading. Nevertheless, a dialogue is realized in the process of interpretation, where a reader orchestrates a dialogue with oneself. In face-to-face dialogue, there is a coincidence of a speaker's intention with the meaning of what is said. In writing, the meaning of what is said breaks away from the writer's intention, and thus has semantic autonomy (see Ricoeur 1976, 29). Writing fixes what is said, inscribes complete thoughts. It is not merely a record of spoken dialogue but instead is often the direct expression of complete thoughts. In the absence of the common situation of face-to-face dialogue, we cannot conveniently use demonstrative pronouns like "this" or "there." What can these pronouns refer to in writing? It is not like someone is there to point to something in the room. In writing, "this" always connects back to previous complete thoughts to interlock the series or concatenation of complete thoughts. In this way, writing and reading enact a cancellation of the immediate here and now of the face-to-face dialogical environment. The speaking and listening enacted in reading occur on the side of only the reader (see Ricoeur 1976, 31).

Our temptation is to think that only the reader—as the one read to, not the one giving voice to the text—listens. But this is a mistake. If the process of interpretation really does involve a second-order dialogue between an "I" and a "Thou" (the reader in two roles), then both parties in the dialogue must listen to one another. In other words, not only do texts speak, they also listen. How so? Through the questions they pose to readers. Readers ask questions of a text, but the text also asks its own questions and asks questions of readers. Texts themselves pose questions to readers. As Gadamer explains, interpreting a text means "that it puts a question to the interpreter ... Interpretation always involves a relation to the question that is asked of the interpreter" (Gadamer 2013, 378). Active reading involves talking back to the text we read. Who is it posing these questions to readers (Dickman 2022a, 45)? Since questions are a mode of listening, who is it that listens to what readers have to say? There obviously are no writers available to hear what we are saying back to them. Books obviously cannot listen. We readers can only speak with ourselves, as the voice of the text and as the one to whom the text is read. The text itself—given voice by the reader—is who listens. A listening text adds to the explosion of the ordinary environment that writing generates. This helps explain why we grasp different meanings when we read the same text. It is not just that we have changed perspectives. It is that the text itself listens to what we have to say, and changes what it says in turn. This is what allows some texts to speak continually with new generations of readers.

Another way writing transforms our immediate environment into a world of meaning is through the alteration of reference. As noted, in face-to-face dialogue we can point to things in our immediate environment to clarify that about which we speak. Imagine having dinner with a friend, and they ask, "Can you pass that to me, please?" What "that" refers to will be clear by an indication such as their eye glance, pointing with their hand, or nodding their head. In writing, however, there is no shared immediate environment between writer and reader. As Ricoeur writes:

> What happens to reference when discourse becomes a text? It is here that writing and above all the structure of the work alter reference to the point of rendering it entirely problematic ... Without a doubt it is this abolition of demonstrative or denotative characteristics of reference which makes possible the phenomenon which we call literature, where every reference to given reality may be abolished. But it is essentially with the appearance of certain literary genres ... that this abolition of reference to the given world is led to its most extreme conditions. It is the role of most of our literature, it would seem, to destroy this world.
>
> (Ricoeur 1974, 79)

If our environment is destroyed, what replaces it? Meaningful worlds. Rather than looking for something pointed at *behind* the book, writing opens the option to reference possibilities *in front* of the text. Writing does not, as Barthes writes, "make people see, it does not imitate; the passion that may consume us upon reading a novel is not that of a 'vision' (in fact, strictly speaking, we 'see' nothing). It is the passion to discover meaning [aka complete thoughts], it is a striving towards a higher relation, which also carries its emotions, its hopes, its threats, its triumphs. What goes on in [writing] is, from the referential (real) point of view, strictly nothing" (Barthes 1975, 271). As we discussed with regard to predication, predicates unlock productive reference in opposition to denotative reference. It is not just that we are alive in the present, but that we are alive in the 2023rd year of the Christian era or in the 2566th year of the Buddhist era. It does not mean there is no reference. Instead, we are freed to a second-order reference to existential possibilities. What kind of existential possibilities unfold in front of the text? Ricoeur calls this "the world of the text" (Ricoeur 1974, 80). Since this is a new or different world from our ordinary immediate environment, the world of the text distances us from ourselves. It is, in other words, "a distanciation of the real from itself" (Ricoeur 1974, 80). This why we can speak of the Greek world, or even the world of Narnia. The world of the text—as a hermeneutic principle—is what makes *all* redescription possible. Understanding the world of the text is obviously not some mere psychic transposition into the mind of a writer. As an analogy, consider fanfiction, how fans build upon underdeveloped aspects of the world of the text.

A third radical change engendered by writing involves a risk, the courage to retrieve meanings on the other side of radical alienation. Recall the illustration about the child throwing a stone into a pond, enjoying the ripples made. The child could see themselves outside themselves. Texts too are a way we understand ourselves outside ourselves. Texts provide semantic laboratory conditions where we are distanced from our ordinary world but return to our lives changed. As Gadamer writes:

> Nothing is so strange, and at the same time so demanding, as the written word ... The written word and what partakes of it—literature—is

> the intelligibility of mind [*geist*] transferred to the most alien medium ... In deciphering and interpreting it, a miracle takes place: the transformation of something alien and dead into a total contemporaneity and familiarity. This is like nothing else that comes down to us from the past. The remnants of past life—what is left of buildings, tools, the contents of graves—are weather-beaten by the storms of time that have swept over them, whereas a written tradition, once deciphered and read, is to such an extent pure mind that it speaks to us as if present. That is why the capacity to read, to understand what is written, is like a secret art, even a magic that frees and binds us. In it time and space seem superseded. People who can read what has been handed down in writing produce and achieve the sheer presence of the past.
>
> (Gadamer 2013, 163)

Writing is an extreme alienation, a total exteriorization of human beings, with nothing resembling us about it. Books do not make sounds like us. Books do not look like or move like us. Books do not live like us. Readers have to make the text speak. In doing this, we grasp meanings that are said in writing from across vastly different cultures and times. These texts speak to us, which is more than just showing us things from the past. Through reading, we make each other present in dialogue.

The distance between us and books is not a literal physical distance. It is, rather, an issue of the otherness definitive of cultural or historical estrangement. The world of the text destroys the given environment because it is so different. Books are aliens alongside us. Or, really, we are aliens to texts. Distanciation like this forms the counterpart to our capacity for appropriation, to make meanings our own (see Ricoeur 1976, 43). We will return to appropriation later. Many cases of alienation we misrecognize, though. For example, many Christians in contemporary US society will state that, "Jesus is King." The problem is that "king" plays no significant role in the lives of democratic—or anti-monarchic—people. That is, "king" makes no genuine sense as a superlative symbol or predicate for their savior or god (see Tillich 2001, 49–50). On a broader level, we can experience alienation from cultural traditions, such as people's resistance to Confucianism and Buddhism after the Communist revolution in China or people's reaction to modern science while attempting to maintain their Christian commitments. And this says nothing about attempting to preserve traditions in the face of colonizing superiority and brutality (see Wiredu 1997). The issue is that interpretation is a risk we take to venture across vast differences of meanings. As Ricoeur writes, "Interpretation, philosophically understood, is nothing else than an attempt to make estrangement and distanciation productive" (Ricoeur 1976, 44). We can undertake this across time, across culture, and even across alienation from ourselves—such as when we understand ourselves or integrate our experiences better by reading our own writing, as growing research in expressive writing therapy for PTSD patients suggests (see Smyth, Hockemeyer, and Tulloch 2008; Baikie, Geerlings, and Wilhelm 2012). We can also point out that reading and deeply interpreting texts even surpasses tourism through foreign countries (see Gadamer 2013, 392). Perhaps you object to this, that of course travelling is grander than just sitting with a book. Yet how can we really appreciate and savor our experience of travelling if we do not simultaneously understand what is said or written about a culture? Like merely reacting to a book instead of reading a text, tourism can often be mere sightseeing than an engagement with others where we broaden our horizons of understanding. We actively read or interpret when we ask questions. This is how we thread lines of thought together into texts we interpret. These worlds of texts transform environments into cultural worlds.

There Are Four Layers of Questions in the Reading Process

Not only do texts ask questions of readers, but active readers must also ask questions of texts. I want to specify four layers of questions that readers ask through interpretation. I develop these layers of questions on the basis of early childhood literacy pedagogy (see Dickman 2022a, 59–76; Raphael 1986; Adler and Van Doren 1972). The first kind of question readers have to ask are what I call "on-the-lines" questions. These focus reader attention on explicit information stated in sentences. Such questions can be answered only by looking at specific sentences in a book. Taking the *Bhagavad Gita* as an example, we can ask, "Where did Arjuna ask Krishna to drive his chariot?" The answer is, "Arjuna asked Krishna to drive his chariot in between the two armies." These are information-seeking or sincere questions, where the reader lacks the information and gains it through the act of questioning. With children, we can tell they are learning to read by whether or not they can answer these sorts of questions. They need to demonstrate they can grasp these basic threads of complete thoughts for fabricating the world of the text. My favorite toddler book, *Brown Bear, Brown Bear, What Do You See?* (Martin and Carle 1967), uses repetition and illustrations to help children acquire this skill of asking and answering on-the-lines questions. The questions and answers are both explicit: Brown bear, what do you see? I see a red bird looking at me. Red bird, what do you see? And so on. Kids can anticipate answers by glancing at the pictures. These questions and answers provide the basic threads for the fabric of the textual world. The reader is prompted to ask, and thus share, the right question, and thus the sentence that answers to that question is transformed into a complete thought understood.

Since books contain series of sentences, readers have to determine what needs more attention and also what is not stated explicitly in any single sentence. Questions that look for implicit complete thoughts are what I call "between-the-lines" questions. This is the second kind of question necessary in interpretation. Through these questions, readers have to infer from explicitly stated complete thoughts what is left unwritten. For example, a character trait might not be stated in a sentence, but readers can infer it through multiple complete thoughts. In the *Lord of the Rings* trilogy, Gandalf has a number of actions and statements attributed to him, and from these a reader might infer that "Gandalf is wise" even though this is not explicitly written in one sentence throughout the books. For another example, maybe some statements seem to contradict one another, and so a reader asks, "How do these statements fit together?" In the first verses of the *Book of Genesis*, the god appears transcendent and all-knowing but just a chapter later this god asks the primordial human beings, "Where are you?" Can an all-knowing god ask a genuine question? If a reader assumes not, then the reader will need to make the question consistent with that perhaps by seeing it as rhetorical rather than sincere. On-the-lines and between-the-lines questions generate the world of the text (cf. Ricoeur 1988, 174).

I call the third layer of questioning "behind-the-lines" questions. These focus readers' attention on details about, for example, a writer's life, historical context of a book, the economic conditions for the book's publication and circulation, and more. Recall that rules or constraints set us free rather than limit us. One constraint on reader caprice is historical context. While there might be some clues about this among the explicit sentences of a book, in many cases we can find most of this information without consulting the book. Sometimes we can detect what era a book is from by its terms, such as when a writer uses the archaic "mankind" for humankind. As Schleiermacher explains, "The vocabulary and the history of the period in which an author [writes] constitute the whole within which [their] texts must be understood with all their peculiarities" (Schleiermacher 1978, 10). Sometimes readers need a sense of how an "original audience" would perceive a book. For example, the New Testament scholar Amy-Jill Levine explains how a lot of contemporary Christian preaching in the US is explicitly or implicitly anti-Jewish because contemporary Christian preachers do not have an adequate grasp on first-century Palestinian Jewish culture (Levine 2015, 20). Jewish stereotypes abound in such preaching, reframing parables as if Jesus and "the Jews" battle, as if Jesus accepts all sinners and Jews reject them (Levine 2015, 23). However, it is not as if the notion of forgiveness was new to Palestinian Jews (Levine 2015, 30–40). Emphasizing how original audiences would have taken Jesus' parables serves as an antidote to pernicious anti-Judaism in contemporary Christian interpretations. Questions about a writer's psychology also go "behind the lines." Some readers of Wittgenstein's works, for example, ask why he writes in such an enigmatic style. The logician Jakko Hintikka suggests this is a result of dyslexia (Hintikka 2000, 6). The original audience, as well as writer psychology, do not really enter our questioning, though. For example, when we perceive the three-dimensional image in an autostereogram (see the Appendix), we do not ask, "What kind of person was the designer?" or "Is this how the original audience would have seen this?" Further still, we can ask about the materiality of the book or other media itself, from the paper quality to the notebook (laptop) design for reading.

The fourth and decisive layer of questioning is what I call "beyond-the-lines" questions. These focus reader attention on ways readers' lives are transformed in light of their dialogue with a text and on ways interpretive communities legitimize some interpretations over others. We can detect these lines of questioning when, for example, what a text says leads a reader to revise their anticipation of meanings (Gadamer 2013, 278–310). Sometimes what a text says to us surprises us, *even when we have already read the book before*. Prejudices lead different readers to weave complete thoughts together in varying ways. This layer of questioning is existential, where a dialogue is achieved between an I and a Thou. Moreover, since questions are not solely in our power, the I and Thou of a reader's interpretive dialogue become a "we" in shared questioning. Just as face-to-face dialogue always is accompanied by an incompleteness because it can always be resumed later, there is an incompleteness to interpretations of texts. Through sustained dialogue with texts, our worlds are transformed. By way of questions beyond the lines, the reader realizes a "fusion of horizons," bridging between the virtual world of the text and the existential world of the reader (see Iser 1972).

These four layers of questioning interlock with the numerous coordinates of questions noted in Chapter 3 on the mediums of interpretation, where I specified these coordinates, such as predicate-centered questions in the domain of single complete thoughts, conclusion-centered questions in the domain of reasoning with multiple complete thoughts, and synthesis-centered questions in the domain of dialectical dialogue. In this way, we can limit questioning in interpretation to between sixteen to thirty-two kinds of questions. Remember, though, that constraints set us free! Like there are eighty-eight keys on a piano, there are a limited number of kinds of questions in interpretation. For example, we can ask predicate-centered on-the-lines questions as well as predicate-centered between-the-lines questions. I am not saying that we *should* ask only these sorts of questions. I am trying to point out that we in fact do only ask these sorts of questions. However, this should make us self-conscious, and perhaps suspicious now. If these are questions we *do* in fact ask in interpretation, are we asking ourselves these questions right now as we read these words? While questions are explicit in children's books like *Brown Bear, Brown Bear, What Do You See?*, they are not explicit for each sentence line in most books or articles. When we teach and test students on reading comprehension, though, we do make these questions explicit for them. Learning to read, or literacy, is our ability to internalize this question-answer dynamic. Helping children learn to read involves slowing down and making explicit these steps of questioning in interpretation.

Classifying questions discretely like this can be a problem, though. Doing so suggests each category of questioning is relevantly distinct from the others. They are intrinsically interconnected. Beyond-the-lines questions obviously require on and between-the-lines questions. However, on-the-lines questions can be just as affected by beyond the lines questions. This mutual implication relates to Fish's point that interpretive communities and institutions of power authorize what counts as a legitimate interpretation. Consider what seems to be a straightforward on-the-lines question: Who are Jesus' disciples (see Dickman 2022a, 67)? The Gospel of John, for example, mentions that there are twelve but does not name all of them. Mark says one is named Thaddaeus, while Matthew and Luke do not use this name but say this is Judas the son of James. The point here is that our answer to the straightforward on-the-lines question involves assumptions we make about how to prioritize the four different canonized gospels. Which one will a reader privilege over the others? Will it be based on which book was written first? This would be to use behind-the-lines questions to narrow the scope of on-the-lines questions. Schleiermacher explains it is more difficult to divide these categories than we might hope. Readers' attitudes affect their anticipations about the "whole" or complete meaning of a text, and their attitudes affect how readers empathize with the speaker in the text (see Schmidt 2006, 16–18). Books and readers are parts of a broader language and culture (see Schleiermacher 1977; Schmidt 2006). On-the-lines and between-the-lines questions are incomplete without the other layers of questioning.

I want to turn to one last point to bring these threads together into a helpful notion of "classic" texts.

Paradigmatic Texts Are Classics

While it is important to challenge the hegemony of the Eurocentric canon of literature, we can still develop a notion of a "classic" text based on the hermeneutic we have developed throughout this text. If classics are tied intrinsically to Eurocentrism and colonial dominance—if labelling a book a "classic" merely reinscribes institutional power—then this notion is not worth salvaging (see Williams 2021; cf. Bloom 1994). We can address this concern by returning to our distinction between books and texts. Have you ever been in a professor's office cluttered with books? Or have you ever been to a person's home where many living spaces are filled or even overflowing with books? Imagine what this signifies to some visitors or undergraduate students. Rather than indicating being well-read, it can function as symbolic capital to indicate belonging to a privileged bourgeoisie class. Fetishization of books is not the same as understanding texts. What is it to call a text, rather than a book, a classic?

A classic text is an achievement that does not become outdated, because it has an unlimited capacity to speak and listen to new generations of readers (see Gadamer 2013, 285). A text like this rises above mere reactive feelings that whimsically change over and over. Recall that elevation is a metaphor for increased freedom. The freedom is to speak with and be heard by more readers. As Gadamer explains, classic texts epitomize the nature of historical being: "preservation amid the ruins of time" (Gadamer 2013, 301). The voices of classic texts speak from the past but not merely about the past; they speak presently to present issues for readers. A classic is not a mere document recording past events. They are not books, mere family heirlooms handed down to us. They are not like a record collection never listened to for fear of scratching them or a comic collection never read for fear of not preserving them. Instead, classic texts—while still handed down—make what is said present or contemporaneous with us (see Gadamer 2013, 408). No matter how many technological advancements we make, we still struggle with forming friendships, with anxiety about mortality, with ethical consumption of animals, and more—some of the very same themes at issue in many classic texts, such as the *Epic of Gilgamesh*.

Returning to the issue of reading the same text twice, most theorists try to explain this by pointing out that readers change over their lives between readings. The text changes because the "I"—or really the self—has changed. Wolterstorff, for example, points out readers gain new insights upon new readings because "each of us at a particular stage in our lives is cognitively privileged with respect to certain facets of reality and cognitively underprivileged with respect to others" (Wolterstorff 1995, 185). As our prejudices and biases change, our interpretations change. This neglects, however, that texts are not inert artifacts, that texts are not books. The same text says different things on different readings because such texts *listen*! I add this to refine further our notion of a classic. Classics are texts with the capacity to listen to what readers have to say (back) to them. We do not simply ask questions about what is on the lines, between them, behind them, and beyond them. As stated earlier, the text itself asks questions of us as readers. Just as every line can be understood as an answer to a question, readers need to ask those explicit and implicit questions, thus sharing them with the text itself (see Booth 1979, 238). The readers listen to what texts say by asking questions proper to the lines of the texts, but texts themselves also listen to what readers have to say in response to what the texts say. Classics like this are the "same" texts addressing the same subject matters but are understood in different ways in light of different reading situations (see Gadamer 2013, 416). What makes the text the "same" is not mathematical equivalence, but semantic integration. We get different things out of the same text because our dialogues with them are ongoing. We are not "done" reading a classic upon just one reading of it. In fact, the four layers of questioning can correspond to levels of "re-reading," where it really takes reading a text four times to interpret it adequately by cycling through each layer of questioning (see Ricoeur 1988, 174; Adler and Van Doren 1972, 16–17). These are layers rather than "kinds" of reading because they accumulate, where second order questioning presupposes first order questioning, and so on.

The accumulation of classics, of cacophonies of voices that continue to engage with us in dialogue, establishes written traditions. Some scholars take a myopic approach to tradition by confusing it with institutions. The feminist theorists Kathleen MacIntosh and Kate Bagley, for example, urge that we must confront and challenge traditions, as if traditions are the loci of domination and oppression (see McIntosh and Bagley 2007, 97). One way to clarify a helpful notion of tradition is to distinguish traditions from institutions. Institutions are necessary for sustaining practices. For example, while basketball as a game is enjoyable, money is required for the maintenance of quality courts and hoops. While players—usually—can focus on goods internal to the practice like a game well played, institutions focus on acquisition of funds, such as ticket sales, construction contracts, etc. Because of this, institutions are dangerous to practices. Their focus and forces are centrifugal to standards of excellence and goods internal to practices (see MacIntyre 1981, 194). Thus, institutions can corrupt practices without critical oversight (see Dickman 2018b). They can turn a sport into a mere spectacle. When institutions take over traditions, what I call the process of institutionalization, a drift occurs away from internal goods (e.g. a game well played) toward external goods (e.g. money)—particularly toward the inequitable distributions of those external goods. In the effort to acquire patronage, protection, and power from elite literati and government officials, early Chan Buddhists emphasized a non-discursive spiritual experience to render their position beyond critique (see McRae 2003, 45; Sharf 1995, 259). This proved strategic in dominating Buddhist institutions throughout China in the medieval era. We know with regard to the political and social determinants of health, for a different example, that Black women in the US are four times more likely to die in childbirth than White women (see Dawes 2020). Many have shown that the medical model or "biologic" theory of race is complicit with white supremacy, pointing out that racism—not "race"—is a determinant of health (see Khazanchi, Evans, and Marcelin 2020). That is, the good that is internal to health care practices (aka well-being) is subordinate to institutionalized white supremacist interests baked into health and legal systems in the US profit-driven economy. Institutionalization restricts and polices power distributions and social hierarchies, and these arrangements take on a veneer of what is normal or natural. Recall our effort to challenge our natural attitude in Chapter 2 on the initiatives of interpretation.

Practices just are traditions from the perspective of a specific moment in time or a synchronic perspective. Traditions, on the other hand, are practices from a perspective spanning over history or a diachronic perspective (see Stout 2005, 135–136). Traditions are accumulated practices, and these have structures that set us free just like the rules of basketball set us free to play it. These have no goals outside themselves. They promote and cultivate growth, where we strive to move beyond our individual limitations, limitations like our propensity to worry anxiously, and to move toward broader horizons for understanding and being. Thus, as Ricoeur explains, traditions include both free innovation and accumulated sedimentation (Ricoeur 1986, 125; see also Gadamer 2013, 292). When people talk about "traditional" cultures, or "traditional" marriage, or the "traditional" god, they associate tradition solely with the sedimented aspect of tradition. The traditions within which we are embedded do not restrict our freedom but rather provide a framework for freedom to happen. They are part of us and move and change with us. That is, just as with consciousness, we cannot make tradition an object for analysis, we cannot objectify tradition to ourselves. According to Gadamer, individualistic hermeneutics like that of neoliberalism or romanticism "conceives of tradition as an antithesis to the freedom of reason and regards it as something historically given, like nature. And whether one wants to be revolutionary and oppose it or preserve it, tradition is still viewed as the abstract opposite of free self-determination, since its validity does not require any reasons but conditions us without our questioning it" (Gadamer 2013, 293). This misconception of tradition prevents us from recognizing that we are a part of the historical flowing of tradition, in which is included both free innovation and settling into patterns.

This is especially the case with the accumulation of texts in written traditions. Each new interpretive situation demands a new interpretation. As Gadamer writes:

> The historical life of a [written] tradition depends on being constantly assimilated and interpreted. *An interpretation that was correct in itself would be a foolish ideal that mistook the nature of tradition.* Every interpretation has to adapt itself to the hermeneutical situation to which it belongs.
>
> (Gadamer 2013, 415; my emphasis)

Interpretations radiate from generations continually engaging with classics. This radiance captivates readers, drawing each of us in for new and renewed readings. Written traditions involve sedimentation into genres as retrospective typologies of composition, but these are not, as Ricoeur emphasizes, "eternal essences" (Ricoeur 1986, 125). When our embeddedness within the currents of traditions attenuates or weakens, we lose our sense of generational succession. For example, today artists are criticized for copying or imitation, when faithful recreation of grandmasters was a cultural achievement in earlier eras. As Gadamer emphasizes, "wherever this law operated as a matter of course it provided freedom for the most individual self-expression" (Gadamer 1980, 9). That is, within the constraints of imitation, students of the masters found freedom. Today, though, we judge imitation as a shortcoming rather than an achievement. We are all supposed to be original artists, original thinkers, or original individuals. This is a weird ahistorical notion of "originality." It indicates a cultural alienation, as if we are radically unique individuals—recall our critique of neoliberal individualism in Chapter 2 on the initiatives of interpretation.

With regard to questions in particular, we can point to numerous ways we are alienated from currents of traditions. We live in an age of answers, overloaded with dogmas about what we are supposed to believe and do. Awash in toxic positivity, we are supposed to "just be yourself" or "do what you feel." Or with commercialization, advertisers constantly tell us what products we need to feel happy or fulfilled. Religious institutions, too, join in on the entire racket. Street preachers ask people who pass by, "Have you accepted Jesus as your messiah (or as your lord and savior)?" This is not really a question. It is telling you what the answer is: Jesus is your messiah. Jesus is your savior. Consider this, though. How many contemporary Christians today live within a culture where it makes sense to ask the question, "Who is my messiah?" That is, first century Palestinian Jews lived under a set of social conditions where the question made sense, where the predicate was part of their field of intelligibility within which to interpret their experience. Can someone really ask this question who does not live within first century Jewish self-understanding? We can change the context for a different example. Many people say that Siddhartha Gautama is the Buddha. Yet what kind of culture is it where "Who is my Buddha?" is a live question? My point here is to challenge naiveté with regard to our accumulation of supposed answers, and to raise a criticism that we are not genuinely asking the questions to which such statements answer. Under the aegis of the hermeneutic priority of questioning, our embeddedness in living traditions rests in our capacity to share questions, not in our collection of answers.

In this chapter, I have argued that the proper objects of interpretation are texts, not books, and that these engage us in dialogue. I also indicated ways writing explosively expands our horizons, opening us to new sorts of dialogue partners and extraordinary references. I developed the four readings or ways of questioning in our engagement with texts, necessary questions we have to ask to acquire literacy. Classics are writings that engage us most thoroughly in this dialogue.

Chapter 5

The Practices of Interpretation

Perhaps some readers are confused about what my text is saying, about what interpretation is and how to do it. How does distinguishing between books as artifacts and texts as voices help us to interpret? How does becoming reflexive about interpretive consciousness support improving our skill at interpretation? How does promoting dialogue relate to our effort to interpret? How does developing a concept of texts as concatenated complete thoughts help focus interpretation? Why does questioning have hermeneutic priority—as we have revisited again and again this throughout this text? I hope that readers can answer these questions rather than experience frustration with them. Just in case, I want to respond to each question briefly. We need to distinguish books and texts in order to specify what we actually interpret: texts, not books. We need to be aware of our positionality as interpreters, being cautious about Eurocentric prejudice especially. We need to focus on dialogue—engaging one another—rather than just decode signs as isolated individuals. We need to hold complete thoughts together under a hierarchy to bring forth the world of the text. Questioning facilitates each of these aspects definitive for interpretation. I want now to bring these threads together more tightly.

This chapter on practices of interpretation will prove to be the most practical, approximating a "how to" approach to interpretation. I want to argue for a few things. I draw out four crucial steps for interpretation: a first impression, a critical explanation, a comprehensive integration of discrete parts into a whole, and an application. I also want to distinguish the product (an interpretation) from the process (interpretation). I focus on appropriation in particular, which is our ability to move from merely considering meanings to taking ownership of them. I close by detailing some features of interpretive communities, emphasizing in particular how communal questioning takes precedent over individuals. This is based on how sharing questions is required for understanding or even appropriating meanings.

The Process of Interpretation Incorporates Explanation and Application as Steps

Interpretation is not a single act that we do to a book, an artifact, or an individual's feeling of empathy for a writer. Naïve neoliberal (rooted in romanticism) hermeneutics insists on this as what counts as an interpretation. If you like it, then buy it! Or really, buy it because we are telling you that you will like it. Instead, interpretation is a process. That is, interpretation is a practice encompassing multiple steps: conjecture, explanation, comprehension, and application (see Ricoeur 1976, 74; Gadamer 2013, 319). As a practice, it is social—which we will get to below in the fourth section of this chapter. For now, I want to isolate each moment of the process. The first moment is the conjecture, a tentative supposition based on incomplete information. Here we try to make a first impression of a text or give a first voice to the text in the absence of the writer. This involves a glance over the text. It may seem to take only reading an abstract or reviewing the table of contents, like watching the trailer to a movie and thinking you have everything you need. It is more than that, though. It is more an educated guess or probability judgment that takes into consideration some relevant information (Hirsch 1967, 170–171). When we see a trailer, for example, we are not merely surveying brief episodes from the movie itself. We also have a sense of the broader genre, the production company, the actors, directors, and producers, as well as related films in a series with prequels and sequels. In this way, we are looking at the trailer or film from a broad range of relevant sides. This happens with texts, too. Before we even start reading, literate people usually can tell if a book is a novel, a math textbook, a children's collection of fables, a philosophical treatise, or what have you.

On a quick skim, we can also detect frequency of specific traits within the text as well as those traits among other texts within a genre. There are no methods for making good, educated guess beyond this broad literacy (see Ricoeur 1976, 76). Before we interpret, we have to have a sense of what is important for increasing the probability of our initial judgment. We use a "first reading" to develop this sense. With regard to question layers specified in the previous chapter on the objects of interpretation, this initial conjecture uses some on-the-lines, between-the-lines, and behind-the-lines questions. However, our inherited prejudices shape our initial questions with anticipations for meanings in or of the text. The tentative or conjectured meanings emerge because we read and question with regard to this initial anticipation of what the text means, how our expected meaning should relate parts with the whole (see Gadamer 2013, 279). In this way, we formulate a predication, but it is not a mere shot in the dark. Unlike romantic or neoliberal hermeneutics that assume a pantheistic metaphysics of individualism, our initial conjecture is not some mere divination of what is in a different individual's mind (see Gadamer 2013, 203).

The second moment is explanation. Here we have to objectify the text, suspending its semantic autonomy and treating it as a structure without some speaking agency (Ricoeur 1976, 81). We have to do this in order to break it down and analyze it into parts that make up the whole. We cannot do an anatomy of a living person, so we should not expect to do this to a speaking and listening text. Whereas we weave threads together in our initial conjecture and in our comprehension, with explanation we unravel the threads (see Hughes and McCutcheon 2022, 96). That is, the primary function of explanation is to take a text apart, to specify and isolate its parts. The explanatory moment helps us increase and refine our evidence to support or—what is even better—falsify our initial conjecture. To explain is, as Ricoeur writes, "to unfold the range of propositions and meanings …" (Ricoeur 1976, 72). Just as with the conjecture, though, these parts need not be solely from within the text. Breaking the text down into parts also involves appeals to what is outside the text, such as the publisher, the historical or political context within which the text was produced, and more. Just as words are parts of a whole sentence, sentences are parts of a whole book. Moreover, books are parts of a culture and historical period.

The explanatory moment incorporates our second and third (re-)readings, with questions about what is between the lines and what is behind the lines (see Dickman 2022a, 73). One especially troubling prejudice many readers have that explanation can critique is anachronism, our tendency to project contemporary or modern concepts onto historically and culturally distant texts. Consider, for example, contemporary debates in US Christianity concerning what their bible teaches about "homosexuality." This concern projects a notion onto first century Palestinians that they simply did not have. Early twentieth century medicine and psychiatry coined this concept along with its inverse "heterosexuality" for pathological obsession with either the same or the opposite sex (see Katz 1995). Taking the text apart might involve determining the authorship of it or how original audiences took it. It might involve breaking down the internal structure of the text using methods in literary criticism, but it might involve breaking down the cultural origins of the text through historical and postcolonial methods. We can also break a text down in terms of implicit (or even explicit) assumptions made about nature or global warming with ecocriticism or those made about gender with feminist critique. Through quantitative methods, we can determine large and relevant numbers of members that belong to a class of interest to us (see Hirsch 1967, 178). I once had access to digitized English versions of Wittgenstein's corpus and could track every instance of his use of the word "love." I could use this to create statistics about significant uses of the term in his works.

The third moment is comprehension, a broad synthesis or *reintegration* of the discrete parts isolated in the explanatory analysis. Just as the initial conjecture postulates or anticipates a whole or complete meaning, this moment of the interpretive process also grasps a whole, but this time it involves the integration of differences (see Ricoeur 1976, 72). It is a complex unity achieved rather than a mathematical identity always already extant. This unity funnels into the voice of the text and bursts forth with something to say to readers and ask of readers. It is here that we engage in open-ended dialogue with the text itself instead of merely resting in smug satisfaction with our own projections or merely distracting ourselves with trivializing explanatory inhibitors to our prejudices.

As I hope you can anticipate, this realization of a dialogue with the voice of the text is brought about by questions beyond the lines. If we remain too tied to our quantitative and explanatory methods, then we treat the text as an instance of general human characteristics, where we objectify the text as a mere trivial remnant of an era. Alternatively, if we assume a superiority to the text as neoliberal or romanticist hermeneutics presuppose, then we coopt what the text has to say to us. We "one-up" the text, as if we know the voice better than it knows itself (see Gadamer 2013, 368). In this moment of comprehension facilitated by beyond-the-lines questions, we need to maintain a respect for and openness to the other of the text, to experience the text as a fellow speaker who really has something to say to us and ask things of us. Recall we do not understand others, but what others have to say to us. Thus, in this third moment of the interpretive process we actually listen to the text and are listened to in turn by the text.

The fourth and culminating moment of the interpretive process is application, the adaptation of a text's speaking to a specific situation. As Gadamer elaborates, this is what makes all interpretation similar to performance of a musical score, actually playing and presenting the song (Gadamer 2013, 321). In such a context, the song played is neither some decoding of signs to grasp a writer's intention nor a subjective whim of the performer. There is a kind of truth to the performance where we can judge the quality of the performance, in whether or not the performer (even if we ourselves are the performer) gets the song correct. It is not "objective" in the sense of the natural sciences modeled on mathematics. This presupposes an objectification of the phenomenon where we stand apart from the situation. Instead, in performing and listening to a song, we are involved, not distanced. Our explanatory methods, in the second step in the interpretive process, can seduce us into treating texts this way, preventing listening to what the texts say to us. Application is what affects our ability to get at a single correct or final interpretation. Application is the locus of our ever-changing circumstances in which we interpret texts. Each particular instance of interpretation involves a new context, thus there can never be a final solution.

Gadamer clarifies this difference by examining a historian of law and a judge's relation to laws, and a biblical archeologist and a preacher's relation to scripture (Gadamer 2013, 335–340). When a historian examines a legal document, they are trying to explain it and show how it is a product of its time. When a judge considers a case, however, the judge must decide how the legal document applies to a particular situation. That is, there is a living relation between the text and the present in the judge. When a biblical archeologist studies a biblical text, they are trying to discover remnants corresponding to what is said to confirm or disconfirm the text's historical accuracy. The preacher, alternatively, attempts to apply a moral or spiritual lesson from the text to a current situation. What these examples show us is that we are addressees of the texts rather than that the texts are mere historical repositories we seek to explain. However, it is not to say that we should forgo explanations. It is that explanation is incorporated into the process of interpretation rather than standing in opposition to it. Application is intrinsic to the process, not a separate optional consequent.

An Interpretation Is a Product of the Process of Interpretation

My analysis of the process of interpretation into discrete steps should not seduce us into believing that these are separable entities. It is not as if we can make a guess about a text and just be done with it. It is not as if we can explain a text without understanding it as a whole. It is not as if we can apply what a text says without comprehension. We might also be seduced into thinking that these four steps, like our four layers of questioning, always have to move in this chronological order. Sometimes these happen nearly simultaneously to the point where if we are not sensitive to the discrete steps, it may seem to us that we are doing all four at the same time. They comprise one unified process, and—while it might be helpful for an *explanation* of interpretation like I am undertaking throughout this text to clarify them separately—they are not separable into independently existing activities. They are all mutually informative (see Blum 2012; Segal 2014).

Ricoeur calls this process of interpretation the "hermeneutical arc" (Ricoeur 1976, 87). We can visualize this as an actual curved line, as part of a circumference of a circle—alluding to the famous notion of the hermeneutic circle (see Schleiermacher 1977). The arc starts with conjecture, moves upward to critical explanation where it plateaus and moves on to complex comprehension, and then moves downward to application. While we can admit that this visualization might be helpful for didactic purposes or as a teaching tool to explain (aka break down) the process of interpretation, we need to resist the temptation to take it as an accurate and complete picture. It is not really an arc, because this suggests interpretation is "complete" with an application. It is as if application is the culmination and fulfillment of the process, that without application an interpretation would be unsatisfactory. Moreover, the image is ahistorical, abstracting the process of interpretation out of our situatedness in time. As we strive toward an interpretation, our circumstances evolve, rendering every interpretation partial. I would say "incomplete," but that would suggest we can have a "complete" interpretation. At best, this can function only as a regulative ideal toward which we strive (see Anderson 1998, 135–136). Circumstances move on before we even finish an attempt at interpreting. The point here is that an "arc" is insufficient for visualizing the process once we bring time into the picture. A spiral seems better, but as a two-dimensional shape, it too is ahistorical. What we need to visualize—if visualization is even necessary or helpful, really—is a hermeneutic *coil*. What happens at the moment of application is that the process *starts over*. It is unclear whether human beings are capable of ushering interpretation through the coil to the very end. Hegel promoted our capacity to reach this goal as "absolute knowledge" (Hegel 1977, 479). With the recognition of our limitations and prejudices, in light of the Kantian critique of all metaphysics, we can resist placating ourselves into believing we have achieved this. It is like a dialogue. Just because we have stopped does not mean we will not pick it up again later.

Within these moments of the hermeneutic coil, there are two additional interlocking coils, like satellites circling planets. The first we can call the exegetical hermeneutic circle (see Dickman 2022a, 41). Exegesis focuses on grasping the internal configuration of a text, as well as the text's broader historical situation. Relations of parts and whole of a text guide this circle, where parts contribute to the interpretation of the whole text and the whole text contributes to the interpretation of its parts. Like sentential subjects and predicates compose whole complete thoughts, complete thoughts change the significance of the subjects and predicates. The same goes for texts. Paragraphs contribute chapters, just as chapters reflect back on those paragraphs. Chapters contribute to the whole text, just as the whole text reflects back on those chapters. Questions about what is on the lines, between the lines, and even those about what is behind the lines facilitate grasping these parts and whole relations within historical context (see Dickman 2022a, 65). The second satellite we can call the existential hermeneutic circle. This focuses on interpreters' dispositions and attitudes as they are refigured through engagement with texts (see Gadamer 2013, 278–310). Readers engage in dialogue with texts, and if successful this dialogue transforms readers' lives by broadening our horizons. Our anticipations and prejudices lead us to put parts and wholes together in peculiar ways, but those prejudices that inhibit understanding should be put at risk through questions that are beyond the lines (see Dickman 2022a, 68). As Gadamer writes, "This constant process of new projection constitutes the movement of understanding and interpretation" (Gadamer 2013, 280).

With all of these interlocking interpretive processes preventing us from completion, how can we hope to make *an* interpretation? We can make use of our typical distinction within projects between the process and the product. How does an artist know when a song, or painting, or poem is finished? Musicians either become sick of playing their same hit over and over for audiences, or they try to improve on their songs by remixing them. Even if we turn to architecture, we know that all buildings require upkeep. This does not entail we should never make products like these. An interpretation is a product too, but it is a text and not a book. That is, *the outcome of the process of interpretation of another text*! As anyone familiar with Jewish sacred writings knows, this continual outpouring of interpretation involves the surplus production of texts—from the Torah to the Prophets and Writings, to the Mishnah, to the Talmud and Midrashim, to contemporary commentaries, and more. More meanings are produced, and more texts are interpreted. This is not the worship of written books. It is about reading and engaging in dialogue, grasping meanings into an interpretation for a moment in time. That is, interlocking meanings produce interpretations, through understanding in light of questionings. The quest for meanings—in the sense of complete thoughts, not in the sense of fulfillment or a personal feeling of purpose—is a way of life. However, just because we understand and consider meanings, or even if we apply meanings, that does not mean we appropriate them and make them our own.

Appropriation Involves Taking Ownership of Meanings

Let us return to the fundamental axiom of philosophical hermeneutics: to understand a question is to ask it, but to understand a complete thought is to understand it as an answer to a question. Recall that to consider a question is to be asking it. There is no potential asking of a genuine question. When we hear another person ask a question and we consider it, we ourselves are then also asking it. That is, appropriating the question is accomplished directly in the "understanding" (loosely speaking) of the question. Consider this question: What are good ways to recover from heartbreak? If you are considering this question—and not merely skimming over the interrogative sentence—then you cannot help but ask it. Instead of it solely being *my* question, it has already transformed into *our* question. The appropriation or making the question your own is nearly undetectable. However, unlike questions, complete thoughts we can understand and consider *without* making them our own. I can listen to what another person has to say, I can listen in light of our shared questions, but what they say is not necessarily something I make my own without some further act on my part. That is, we can approach considering what others say in an experimental laboratory, a field of imaginative possibilities. We can understand a meaning without meaning it.

To appropriate another's complete thoughts, we have to reach an agreement with them. Agreement can be explicit, such as when we say, "He speaks for me too," or "I agree with that," or similar phrases. In meetings, people will say, "I second the motion." In these cases, we are not merely taking over the content of what is said but appropriating the discourse more wholly. As Wolterstorff explains, "One's own discourse is a function of that other person's discourse" (Wolterstorff

1995, 52). There is a difference in the content, so it cannot be just the content that is appropriated. For example, if someone says, "I commit to antiracist work," and I say, "Me, too!" I am not saying that I commit *them* to antiracist work. I am saying that I also commit *myself* to it, just like they are committing themselves to it. What is fascinating about a case like this is that not only am I appropriating the predicate (part of the content) but appropriating the disposition toward it (a desire to fulfill the content), too. In this way, we take responsibility for it.

I want us to hesitate here for a moment. So far, it seems like appropriation is an individual's decision, a personal "subjective" choice, or intentional conscious questing for fulfillment. However, when we reach connections with others like this beyond merely sharing questions, our intentionality is, as Levinas writes, "inverted from a failed experience into a beyond experience, into a transcendence, whose rigorous determination is described by ethical attitudes and exigencies, and by *responsibility*, one of the modalities of which is language" (Levinas 1998, 71; my emphasis). Transcendence—on the other side of the Kantian destruction of metaphysics—must be something other than a reference to supernatural entities. Levinas here proposes that transcendence is responsibility. For him, responsibility with and for others and ourselves inverts intentionality. We only embody our connection with others in responsibility, not in some empathetic reconstruction of them or transcendent divination, as in neoliberal or romanticist hermeneutics. And language—dialogue—is a modality of our responsibility with one another (see Dickman 2022c). As the phenomenologist Gail Weiss writes about our responsibility with texts,

> By taking up the responsibility of reading this text as an absolute responsibility, you are making the sacrifice of not fulfilling your responsibility to other texts, other people, other activities. By writing this book, I am making the sacrifice of not writing another book, of not helping others who may be illiterate and therefore unable to engage with this text at all. According to Derrida, "whether I want to or not, I can never justify the fact that I prefer or sacrifice any one (any other) to the other" ... At every moment of life, individuals silently (or not so silently) make unjustified sacrifices, in the name of responsibility, to an other or others, and expect others to do the same for them.
>
> (Weiss 2008, 59)

This responsibility is not an obligation, but an opportunity. To experience this responsibility as a burden is to experience it under neoliberal individualist ideology where "freedom" just is being able to do whatever we want, as if our wants are not infiltrated by consumerism.

What is the opportunity here? It is the opportunity to broaden our horizons. This happens within what Gadamer calls the "fusion of horizons" (Gadamer 2013, 317). It involves reaching agreement on a subject. A possibility for a fusion of horizons is opened up for us when we achieve sharing questioning. Shared questioning melts or liquefies the rigidity of our prejudices. As Gadamer writes, "against the fixity of opinions, questioning makes the [sentential subject] and all its possibilities fluid" (Gadamer 2013, 376). In light of shared questions, we can consider possible predicates for a subject, those that the questions expose as radiating from the subject. Agreement is when we determine shared predicates for that subject. By virtue of shared questioning, I can try these predicates out—weigh them, test them, try them on and take them off, and so on. When a predication works, it expands my horizon and enriches my world. When we share those predicates, we fuse horizons.

Another dimension of appropriation with writing in particular has to do with the productive distance we must cover through interpretation. Recall that nothing is so strange and alien to us as the written word. Texts speak to us, but in very few other respects do they share similarities with us. Writing is the greatest exteriorization of our thinking, as I noted through discussion of Malcolm X, Hegel, classical Chan, and Ibn Rushd in the Preface. As Ricoeur writes, "Reading is the *pharmakon*, the 'remedy,' by which the meaning of a text is 'rescued' from the estrangement of distanciation and put in a new proximity, a new proximity which suppresses and preserves the cultural distance and includes the otherness within the ownness" (Ricoeur 1976, 43). Reading is an otherness within our ownness—the otherness is the voice of the text, and the ownness is its suturing with our own reading voice. Reading itself is a form of appropriation, restoring thoughts to ourselves in resuscitating voices of texts. Through this exteriorization and appropriation facilitated by writing and reading, and through our achievement of shared predicates in response to shared questioning, our lives are reconfigured existentially.

Interpretation Is a Social Practice Not an Individual's Act

Scholars and students of the Christian Reformation in modern Europe know well Martin Luther's criticisms of the Church institution in Western Europe during his time. One of his positions goes by the Latin *sola scriptura*, or scripture alone. It is a principle about the text, that what it says can stand on its own for its intelligibility (see Grondin 1994, 40). The Spirit, or third person of the Christian Trinity, provides the light for this intelligibility for the individual. That is, a person interprets scripture through faith. Scripture is its own key, for Luther. This is what he wielded, as the philosopher Jean Grondin states, "against tradition and the Church's magisterial establishment" (Grondin 1994, 40). The established institution was for licensed representatives of the Church, such as priests, to give interpretations to congregants. In fact, even today many Catholic congregants joke that they have never even read the Christian Bible themselves. Luther saw the institution as providing corrupt or even incorrect interpretations and applications to congregants, leading to his effort to translate the Bible into German and making it accessible to more readers. It is easy to point out the flaws in this, suggesting that someone can just pick up a book and read it for themselves on their own. If the individual can make the text say whatever they want, and can appeal to faith through the Spirit for their interpretation, then any variety of interpretation is legitimate. This has led to the point of what I call the Magic 8 Ball method of reading the Christian Bible, where a person flips through the pages—seemingly at random—and letting them land on a page, feeling that they are opening themselves to a coded or direct message from their god (Dickman 2022a, 162). This is surely compatible for neoliberal consumption. Yet there are also plenty congregants today who rely on an institutional authority (or authoritarian) to tell them what the text says.

Both of these extremes miss the target. Interpretation—or reading—is a social practice. Interpretation is a social cooperative activity with standards of excellence or regulative ideals (see MacIntyre 1981, 187). Participation in it involves comportment to and adoption of those standards in order to realize goods internal to it. Our power to undertake this practice can also extend through transfer to further experiences. Practices direct our attention and effort toward specific goods and goals, and the measure of our excellence is how our actions relative to the practice stand up to precedents. Recall that goods internal to a practice are intangible, like a game well played, compared to external goods that are the focus of institutions, such as money. In fact, the intelligibility of our actions rests on the backdrop of the practice within which they are fitting ones. We can dribble a ball outside the context of a basketball game, but the practice or game of basketball is what grants intelligibility to dribbling. Just so with interpretation. We can sit in front of a book, and even identify things the text is saying, but the process and practice of interpretation grants intelligibility to these actions. There really are not acts or behaviors independent of broader settings. When we explain what someone is doing or saying, and thereby attempt to understand what they are doing or saying, we are writing a narrative history involving their actions with regard to the practice in which it takes place (see Macintyre 1981, 208). These practices, considered historically, are traditions. They provide context for our understanding and orient us toward the future. To participate in a practice well requires a sense of tradition. Just as it takes shared questioning together to fuse horizons together, in our shared questioning we interpret together. Interpretation is not an individualistic thing, but a social practice with organizing principles—those we laid out in elaborating the features of dialogue. Interpretation is, as Gadamer writes, "to be thought of less as a subjective act than as participating in an event of tradition, a process of transmission in which past and present are constantly mediated" (Gadamer 2013, 302). So Luther was wrong. There really is no such thing as an individual's ability to read a text by oneself. This activity is always already embedded in a larger social context of practice and tradition, properly conceived. Individualism and "sola scriptura" themselves become traditions, horizons within which people practice interpretation!

We must be cautious, here, though. As much as practices instill a sense of tradition, institutions instill a sense of hierarchical power. As the scholar of religions Catherine Bell explains, an action is not simply a terminal expression of an intelligible intention with reference to a broader narrative, but also the inauguration of a new situation constraining the field for possibilities of activity (Bell 2009, 72). Consider the fitness industry: we exercise to "get in shape." However, this institutional dynamic is not focused solely on shaping our physical form, but more so focused on constraining cultural possibilities. Consider how patriarchal institutions prevent women's cultural expression and development. As Irigaray writes, "Patriarchal power is organized by submitting one genealogy to the other ... The masculine line of filiation ... doesn't symbolize the woman's relationship to her mother" (Irigaray 2007, 8–9). The genealogy industry and institutions had not symbolized matrilineal filiations very often, though this is changing somewhat in many cultures. Irigaray uses this problem to underscore in addition that male divine symbols inhibit female spiritual projection. Without feminine divine symbols, like feminine genealogies, women's ability to develop subjective or spiritual possibilities is inhibited by these institutions (Irigaray 2007, 11). Institutions generate socialized bodies, structuring dispositions in relation to environments in which these operate (see Bourdieu 1990, 52).

According to Bell, all institutionalizing activities have four features. They are, "situational [contextually specific]; strategic; embedded in a misrecognition of what [they are] in fact doing; and able to reproduce or reconfigure a vision of the order of power in the world, or what I call 'redemptive hegemony'" (Bell 2009, 81). Practices are strategic because, in them, we coordinate *expedient* means for the sake of attaining urgent practical ends. Through these institutional strategies, we differentiate sets of activities from others, often making value-laden distinctions between them. Bell's note about "misrecognition" expands on activity as simultaneously ending and beginning. She references Michel Foucault's argument that while people might know what they are doing and while they might know why they are doing it, "they do not know what what they are doing does" (Bell 2009, 108). In other words, we conceive of ourselves responding within a place to an event, and think our responses as the natural or appropriate thing to do. However, we do not see that we actively create the place and event; we do not recognize how our own actions, in Bell's words, "reorder and reinterpret the circumstances so as to afford the sense of a fit among the main spheres of experience—body, community and cosmos" (Bell 2009, 109).

We believe our responsibilities correspond solely to our intentions. However, we are also responsible for "unintended" consequences. Practices are hegemonic in that they are a lived ordering of power relations which we reproduce, renew and resist through our actions. The redemptive hegemony of practices describes, for Bell, the way in which we experience reality as a "natural" weave of constraint and possibility—the way in which we experience "the fabric of day-to-day dispositions ... as a field for strategic action" (Bell 2009, 84). Redemptive hegemony does not reflect reality, but is its more or less effective creation. To analyze practice in terms of redemptive hegemony is to formulate the unexpressed assumptions that constitute the participant's strategic and expedient conception of the place, purpose, and trajectory of the action. These provide us with a sense of institutional actions or sense of ritual, whereby we deploy power (Bell 2009, 107). This is just as important as our sense of tradition, our sense of humor, our sense of direction, and even our common sense. Such structuring of our social bodies enables us to do things such as whipping together a last-minute birthday party or coordinating a funeral service. Our practical life in relation with institutionalization generate our sense of strategy for negotiating power relations structuring our worlds. This all applies just as much to interpretation. Consider how expedient it is when people say, "Oh, that is just your interpretation." This is dismissive, and a convenient way to shut down dialogue and criticism, but is not rooted in a thoroughgoing philosophy of interpretation. Shutting down discourse takes strategic precedence over accuracy about interpretation. Or consider how *sola scriptura* leads to people interpreting religious texts whatever way they want—"want" being the leverage for late capital profiteering.

Interpretive communities create institutions and establish canons of acceptability (see Fish 1980, 394). Recall that institutions have a corrupting impact on practices and traditions. Canons of acceptability can be ways we lobby for symbolic capital, where institutional authorities deem some interpretations worthy of recognition but not others. Given the global impacts of Eurocentrism, white supremacy informs our institutional legitimacy marginalizing and silencing some voices. Who has the right to interpret? Who has the right to deem some interpretations illegitimate? We must be careful about these questions because "rights" discourse is fundamentally liberal, rooted in Eurocentric individualism—the very philosophy Angela Davis warns is complicit with neoliberal oppression. These pseudo-questions also function as conversation-stoppers, asked in an attitude of a shrug, licensing reader reactive caprice. They are pseudo-questions in these cases because they imply their own answer. Supposedly, "no one" has the right or authority to say one interpretation is correct and another is not. Recall that I have promoted shared questioning and considering responses to those shared questions. By focusing on shared genuine questioning, we change the terms of the conversation but keep it going.

Through reflexivity about our interpretive positions, we continually develop more and more critical cooperative perspectives. When we scan across methods in scriptural criticism, classical approaches include historical and source criticism, and these expand into social-scientific and rhetorical criticism (see McKenzie and Haynes 1999). Overturning these classical and expansive perspectives, we also have ideological criticism, postcolonial criticism, and more. Queer theory in particular challenges heteronormative and homonormative regimes of gender and sexuality imposing and institutionalizing structures on our social bodies (see Thiem 2014, 51). Each of these can be specified by their key questions. Ecocriticism, for example, asks questions concerning a text's assumptions about climate change and nature. As Kwok points out, there is no universal reader, and thus no universal norm for judging these competing methods (Kwok 2016, 8). Moreover, history is replete with forms of hermeneutics besides white supremacist or Eurocentric forms. For example, the Hebrew Bible scholar Jacqueline Vayntrub demonstrates that rather than imposing contemporary literary terms on ancient texts, we need to allow these texts to reveal their own ancient genres, such as in the imaginative language we label as "biblical poetry" (Vayntrub 2019). What this reveals is that Eurocentric scholars often anachronistically project concepts and categories back through time onto ancient texts whose methods themselves challenge supremacist assumptions. For example, asking of early Buddhist Jataka Tales about the Buddha's former lives whether these tales are historical or fictional imposes our concepts of "history" and "fiction" onto them. The same applies when we ask whether New Testament gospels are "factual" or "fictional." The writers and audiences did not have investment in this distinction. Alternatively, the ancient Buddhist strategy of *upaya* or skill of means opened pathways for pluralities of interpretations (see Gummer 2020). This strategy emphasizes the Buddha as a genius teacher, such that he could disseminate different messages to different people with the same single statements. That is, in a single speech, he reaches everyone where they are at, thus there is—and has always been—a diversity of interpretations. There is no need to reinvent the wheel. We have inherited all of these communities of inquiry and interpretation. However, surely there are more options yet to be imagined and put into practice.

These varieties of interpretive communities and frameworks lead to uneasiness among conservative fundamentalists, where they see their book—whether it is the US Constitution or the Quran or the Christian Bible—as inerrant, without any errors. In light of these traditions and institutions for interpretation, Fish writes, "Disagreements cannot be resolved by reference to the facts [of what is right there "in" the text], because the facts emerge only in the context of some point of view ... What is at stake in a disagreement is the right to specify what the facts can hereafter be said to be" (Fish 1980, 338). As Kwok urges, multiple interpretations do not necessarily lead to relativism, but an awareness of our own prejudices (Kwok 2016, 9). This allows us to enter into genuine dialogue with one another, respecting one another, while also taking responsibility for our interpretations instead of deflecting our responsibility to some institutional authorities, divine revelation, or individualistic whims.

In this chapter, I argued that the hermeneutic coil models the interpretive process—from conjecture, through explanation, to comprehension—better than the image of an arc or circle. I also emphasized that an interpretation, as the product of the process, is further production of texts in dialogue with one another. I additionally argued that transitioning from merely considering complete thoughts or meanings to owning them involves responsibility as a modification of intentionality. I also argued that diverse critical approaches to interpretation consist of different kinds of questioning inherited by and definitive for interpretive communities.

Conclusion

What Lies beyond Interpretation?

How can I conclude a text about the hermeneutic priority of questioning? Is a conclusion even appropriate? I do not believe that I have provided all the answers about interpretation, but I hope I provided some guidance toward asking fitting questions and toward questioning in fitting ways. In sum, interpretation of texts moves from conjecture, through criticism, to comprehension of the world of the text, under the regulation of shared questioning in dialogue with the voice of the text and our communities of inquiry, in such a way that we put our prejudices at risk to open ourselves to broadening our horizons. I want to use this space of the conclusion to fashion a function for philosophical hermeneutics in contestations over religious studies theory. Where does interpretation fit in? I also want to reiterate one more time that meaning is proper to discourse, and to emphasize that this constraint is liberating.

Philosophical Hermeneutics Infiltrates Religious Studies Contestations over Theory

Over the last thirty years, a growing contingent of philosophers of religions have advocated both for the relevance of religious studies for better quality philosophy of religions and for the value of philosophy for the academic study of religions (see Anderson 1998; Klemm and Schweiker 2008; Knepper 2013; Schilbrack 2014; Lewis 2016; Dickman 2018b). These scholars recognize that institutionalized philosophy of religion—as it is practiced in Anglo-American universities in philosophy departments—suffers from three shortcomings that decontextualize it from its potential for fruitful cross-disciplinary work (see Schilbrack 2014, 3). First, institutionalized philosophy of religion is narrow. It tends to focus primarily—and often even exclusively—on Christian monotheistic doctrines. Most academics outside of philosophy know that when they hear about philosophy of religion they are preparing to be confronted by Christian apologetics or militant atheistic reactions to those arguments. Of course, doing apologetics belongs in the pulpit, not in the liberal arts classroom. Instead, teaching and learning *about* it in the classroom could work as a topic of study. But *doing* apologetics? That is something for outside the classroom. Second, institutionalized philosophy of religion is intellectualistic because it tends to focus nearly exclusively on religious propositions or doctrine, or purportedly *religious* experience, interpreting these and attempting to determine their truth. Just like language is not a pile of signs, however, religions are not merely sets of confessional claims about transcendent entities but involve social practices, cultural traditions, economic development or turnover, and more.

Third, and most fascinating for my purpose, institutionalized philosophy of religion is insular, walling itself off from the help of diverse methods and theories in religious studies in particular. As an area studies or field rather than a distinctive discipline, religious studies is intrinsically interdisciplinary. Philosophy department insularity makes department members do peculiar and academically suspect things. For example, a professor of Buddhist philosophy at a state university says he wants students to study "Buddhism" (without any qualification or specification to a tradition or sect such as Soto Zen or Thai Theravadin Buddhism) from "the inside," where students will "[glean] religious truths from it for their own lives" (Cherry et al. 2001, 286). This would not pass for academic in a religious studies classroom. Can you imagine a philosopher of religion in Christianity attempting to pray with students in the classroom? Thus, institutionalized philosophy of religion makes itself myopic when neglecting and misrecognizing its limits. Moreover, academic philosophers have a propensity to fetishize founding figures, philosophical schools, or even key topics, like fanboys on Twitter. You might hear one say, "I'm a Plantingian," or see another make a poll about what philosopher is the best. These three shortcomings make philosophy of religions an easy target for rejection by fellow religious studies scholars, some of whom have gone so far as to call for the abolishment of philosophy of religion in religious studies (see Schilbrack 2014, chs. 4–6). If philosophy of religion is this narrow, intellectualistic, and insular, then we might agree to this.

Simultaneously, critics express suspicion about the role "religious literacy" discourse has in religious studies (see Wolfart 2022; Lewis 2016). The religious studies scholar Stephen Prothero advocates for religious literacy in the US because—despite being one of the most religious countries in the world—people in the US know hardly any information about different religions, even their own (see Prothero 2008). Prothero writes, "faith is almost entirely devoid of content" in the US (Prothero 2008, 2). Whether Buddhists, Christians, Muslims, Jews, or still others, people in the US cannot demonstrate knowledge of basic facts about their own religion. A Pew Research Center project on religious knowledge in the US from 2010 showed a surprising result: self-identifying evangelical Christians are among the least knowledgeable about religion, and self-identifying atheists often demonstrated the greatest accurate knowledge. (see Dickman 2020, 221–222). Is knowledge of facts about religions what defines one's religiosity? The religious studies scholar Thomas A. Lewis points out a paradox with Prothero's and others' popular religious literacy projects: "if those who are deeply 'religious' have so little 'religious' knowledge, then we ought to wonder whether 'religious' refers to the same thing in both halves of the [clause]" (Lewis 2016, 121). What it means to be religious to many people might have little to do with retaining facts about their religion's history or founder or scriptures. Perhaps it has more to do with how one votes on candidates with positions about abortion.

While Prothero's intent is to help cultivate knowledgeable citizens who can approach and work with others across our differences, this assumption about "religions" consisting foremost of factual aspects (like a founder or scripture) leaves us, Lewis writes, "dramatically unprepared to comprehend the myriad, complex ways that religion functions in people's lives" (Lewis 2016, 122). Even if atheists are more knowledgeable about the facts, religious people seem inoculated against losing their faith over whether they have accurate information. That is, pointing out to someone that they are incorrect about their own religion actually backfires on the critic. Militant atheists like Richard Dawkins and even scholars like Prothero abstract religions from their living context and dynamism, where someone like Prothero purportedly knows a person's religion better than they themselves know their own religion. What is particularly worrisome is when these abstract constructs shape religious studies curriculum, perhaps in a set of offerings like "Intro to Buddhism," "The Christian Tradition," and others. There is no reason to grant these categories a privileged place in an analysis of the cultural phenomenon going by "religions." Rather than prioritizing facts about a religion we can get to know actual people living out their claims to be religious. That is, our attention turns away from people to Platonic or mystified entities when we study these abstractions like "Islam" or "Indigenous Religions."

The promotion of religious literacy also makes assumptions about "literacy." We know the term has been taken up in a late capitalist jargon, replacing the word "study," such as with media literacy, financial literacy, health literacy, religious literacy, and more. What advance is supposed to be made with the term literacy as opposed to the standard "media studies" or "health sciences" (see Wolfart 2022)? What about "literacy studies" being replaced by "literacy literacy"? When focused exclusively on our ability to read and write for the sake of (economic?) success, literacy has associations with European Christian Empire and colonialism whereby purported "savages" were domesticated into second-class citizens (see Matusov and St. Julien 2004, 203). As literacy studies scholar Harvey J. Graff indicates, there is only a tenuous relation between improved literacy and improved society, by whatever social measures whether economic, legal, or other (Graff 2010, 640). The point is, being able to read and write does not necessarily make us better people.

What I have urged throughout this text is not literacy for its own sake or for leveraging and managing neoliberal exploitation more effectively. Instead, I have urged the hermeneutic priority of shared questioning. This facilitates literacy, but also occurs in oral/aural discourse. Shared questioning helps us achieve communal understanding. I have only employed the world religions paradigm heuristically, without having us commit to the existence of some abstract entities like this or that religion. Like Lewis and Schilbrack advise, we need to engage research participants to get a grasp on lived religion. We use questioning to do this. While we might be tempted to reject my approach to interpretation along with "religious literacy," I hope I have convinced readers that my approach is sufficiently distinct from this.

In attempting to isolate the special place of philosophy for religious studies, Schilbrack develops a visual model of a "Y" structure for coordinating the contestations between or among those who promote description, those who promote explanation, and those who—like Schilbrack—seek to make space for philosophy's role as "evaluation" (see Schilbrack 2014, 179–180). Rather than infighting, this structuring should help religious studies scholars bridge our differences and work together. For Schilbrack, phenomenology and hermeneutics are methods proper to the first level at the bottom of the Y structure, where these enable us to provide a thick description of phenomena that takes into consideration the first-person point of view (Schilbrack 2014, 183). Social scientific methods like psychology and sociology provide explanations in terms of relevant causes, and this forms one of the limbs of the Y structure. Only philosophy can properly assess and evaluate both first-order religious discourse and second-order explanations of religious or cultural phenomena, and this belongs to the other upper-limb of the Y structure. The elegance of this proposal is that neither of the limbs are subordinate to the other, and neither have to do the other's job to complete their main project, yet both must rely on the stem to provide data for explanation and evaluation.

I have two responses to Schilbrack that I hope reframe this organization while simultaneously preserving its strengths. First, just like the circle and spiral, the Y structure can be ahistorical, in that it does not recognize the process of interpretation moving through time. Recall our discussion of the hermeneutic coil in Chapter 5 on the practices of interpretation. As soon as we reach an apparent culmination of the interpretive process in application, we actually start the process over again. This is our lot as historically affected beings. Let us look more closely at correlations between the coil and Schilbrack's Y model. What else is description than the preliminary conjecture? Obviously explanation corresponds with, well, explanation in the hermeneutic coil. And while on the surface evaluation might not seem to correlate with appropriation, what else would we do when we disclose truths? It is not enough to just consider truths. Truth is all of ours. As the critical pedagogical theorist Paulo Freire writes, "There are insistent questions that we all have to ask and that make it clear to us that it is not possible to study simply for the sake of studying" (Freire 2001, 73). Questions open us to receive truths that we discover. Thus, Schilbrack's Y scaffold is better conceived of as spokes on a wheel, the ever-turning hermeneutic coil.

This leads to my second point. If phenomenological hermeneutics as developed throughout this text correlates with Schilbrack's metadiscourse about the competing discourses in religious studies, if the Y structure is actually an axel, then we really cannot relegate phenomenological hermeneutics solely to description. That is, phenomenological hermeneutics infiltrates the metadiscourse on contestations about how to do religious studies properly. Description is done better by ethnography and journalistic reports. Philosophical hermeneutics is not merely relevant to the level of description in religious studies, but to the ever-rotating process of dialogue that constitutes religious studies in the effort to describe, explain, assess or evaluate, redescribe, and so on. I am not advancing philosophical hermeneutics as the new king of the sciences, though, as if I am somehow replacing theology after its displacement by modern science as constructions of medieval intellectual history construe it. Instead, I am saying—as the critic of Orientalism Edward Said explains—since interpretation is everywhere, we cannot help but undertake phenomenological hermeneutics in our work (Said 1997, 162–168).

Restricting Understanding to Discourse Is Liberating

I want to conclude merely by reminding us to keep understanding, and interpretation in particular, humble. Our inclination is to smear understanding across everything, where we expect and demand all things real and unreal, all things natural and supernatural, be understood. My point is that we are unwilling to understand that we are unable to understand most things and mislead ourselves about this. Recall that we can understand discourse only, no more and no less. To specify even further, we can understand only discourse that answers to questions we ourselves are actually asking. We do not understand other people, but what they say. When we focus on the person, we objectify them, silencing their voice as a contributor to the dialogue that we are. So, my encouragement to humble and even restrain our expectations for understanding liberates us to respect one another rather than assimilating others through some neoliberal condescending empathy. By reducing our expectations, we also reduce our disappointment—our existential angst over what we should have already known were lost causes. It is not really that they are lost causes, though. They were never causes to undertake in the first place. We do not understand ourselves or others; we understand what we and others have to say. We do not understand experience; we undergo it, and it evokes in us a need to speak about it. Keeping these domains of life separate liberates us to understand what can be understood. They stimulate our curiosity to question and produce discourse in answer to those questions. Returning to Freire, "Curiosity as restless questioning, as movement toward the revelation of something hidden, as a question verbalized or not, as search for clarity, as a moment of attention, suggestion, and vigilance, constitutes an integral part of the phenomenon of being alive" (Freire 2001, 37–38). Questioning and understanding in a disposition of curiosity is an essential part of living.

May we have the serenity to accept what we cannot understand, the courage to understand what we can, and the wisdom to know the difference.

Appendix

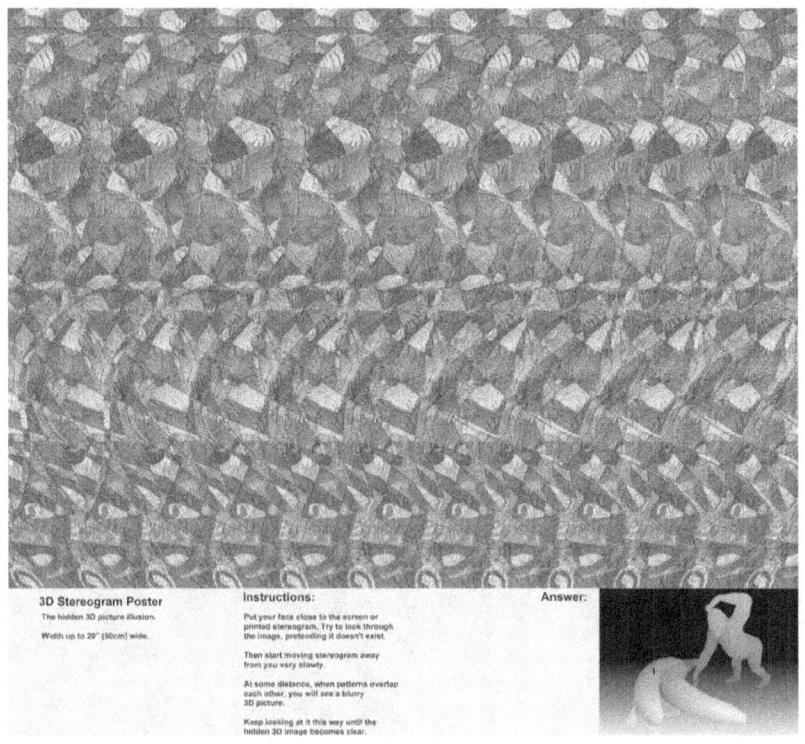

Figure 1. Imagine by 3Dimka/Shutterstock.com.

Further Reading

Voices in Philosophical Hermeneutics

Gadamer, Hans-Georg. (2007). *The Gadamer Reader: A Bouquet of the Later Writings*. Edited by Richard E. Palmer. Evanston, IL: Northwestern University Press.
Gadamer, Hans-Georg. (2013). *Truth and Method*, 2nd revised edition. Translated by Joel Weinsheimer and Donald G. Marshall. London: Bloomsbury.
Ricoeur, Paul. (1976). *Interpretation Theory: Discourse and the Surplus of Meaning*. Fort Worth, TX: Texas Christian University Press.
Ricoeur, Paul. (2003). *The Rule of Metaphor*. Translated by Robert Czerny. London: Routledge Classics.
Schleiermacher, Friedrich. (1977). *Hermeneutics: The Handwritten Manuscripts*. Edited by Heinz Kimmerle. Translated by James Duke and Jack Forstman. Missoula, MT: Scholars Press.

Voices on the Hermeneutic Priority of Questioning

Dickman, Nathan Eric. (2021). *Using Questions to Think: How to Develop Skills in Critical Understanding and Reasoning*. New York: Bloomsbury.
Dickman, Nathan Eric. (2021). "The Hermeneutic Priority of Which Question? A Speech Act Clarification for Interlocutionary Acts." *Informal Logic* 41(3): 485–508.
Freire, Paulo. (2001). *Pedagogy of Freedom: Ethics, Democracy, and Civic Courage*. Translated by Patrick Clarke. Lanham, MD: Rowan and Littlefield Publishers.
Raphael, Taffy E. (1986). "Teaching Question Answer Relationships, Revisited." *The Reading Teacher* 39(6): 516–522.

Voices on Hermeneutics in Religious Traditions

Dickman, Nathan Eric. (2022). *Philosophical Hermeneutics and the Priority of Questions in Religions: Bringing the Discourse of Gods and Buddhas Down to Earth.* New York: Bloomsbury.

Gummer, Natalie. (2020). The Scandal of the Speaking Buddha: Performative Utterance and the Erotics of the Dharma." In Rafal K. Stepien (ed.), *Buddhist Literature as Philosophy, Buddhist Philosophy as Literature*, pp. 197–239. Albany, NY: SUNY Press.

Kwok Pui-lan. (2016). "Reading the Christian New Testament in the Contemporary World." In Margaret Aymer et al. (eds.), *The Gospels and Acts: Fortress Commentary on the Bible Study Edition*, pp. 5–30. Minneapolis, MN: Augsburg Fortress Publishers.

Lopez, Donald S., Jr. (ed.). (1988). *Buddhist Hermeneutics.* Delhi: Motilal Banarsidass Publishers.

Sells, Michael. (2007). *Approaching the Qur'an: The Early Revelations*, 2nd edition. Ashland, OR: White Cloud Press.

Smith, Mitzi J. (2017). *Insights from African American Interpretation.* Minneapolis, MN: Fortress Press.

St. Clair, Raquel A. (2008). *Call and Consequences: A Womanist Reading of Mark.* Minneapolis, MN: Fortress Press.

Tirosh-Samuelson, Hava, and Aaron W. Hughes. (2015). *Michael Fishbane: Jewish Hermeneutical Theology.* Boston, MA: Brill.

Vayntrub, Jacqueline. (2019). *Beyond Orality: Biblical Poetry on Its Own Terms.* New York: Routledge.

Wansbrough, John. (2004). *Quranic Studies: Sources and Methods of Scriptural Interpretation.* New York: Prometheus Books.

Wolterstorff, Nicolas. (1995). *Divine Discourse: Philosophical Reflections on the Claim that God Speaks.* New York: Cambridge University Press.

References

Adler, Mortimer J., and Charles Van Doren. (1972). *How to Read a Book: The Classic Guide to Intelligent Reading*, revised edition. New York: Touchstone.

Adorno, Theodore. (1955). *Prisms*. Translated by Shierry Weber Nicholsen and Samuel Weber. London: Neville Spearman.

Adorno, Theodore. (2003). *The Culture Industry: Selected Essays on Mass Culture*. Edited by J. Bernstein. New York: Routledge Classics.

Ahmed, Sara. (2006). *Queer Phenomenology: Orientations, Objects, Others*. Durham, NC: Duke University.

Anderson, Pamela Sue. (1998). *A Feminist Philosophy of Religion: Rationality and Myths of Religious Belief*. Oxford: Wiley Blackwell.

Anderson, Pamela Sue. (2001). "Gender and the Infinite: On the Aspiration to Be All There Is." *International Journal for Philosophy of Religion* 50: 191–212.

Aristotle. (1999). *Nicomachean Ethics*, 2nd edition. Translated by Terrance Irwin. Indianapolis, IN: Hackett.

Aristotle. (2014). *Complete Works of Aristotle, Volume 1 and 2: The Revised Oxford Translation*. Edited by Jonathan Barnes. Princeton, NJ: Princeton University Press.

Asad, Talal. (2008). "On Suicide Bombing." *The Arab Studies Journal* 15(2)/16(1): 123–130.

Aslan, Reza. (2011). *No god But God: The Origins, Evolution, and Future of Islam*, updated edition. New York: Random House.

Ayoub, Mahmoud M. (2004). *Islam: Faith and History*. London: Oneworld.

Baikie, Karen A., Liesbeth Geerlings, and Kay Wilhelm. (2012). "Expressive Writing and Positive Writing for Participants with Mood Disorders: An Online Randomized Controlled Trial." *Journal of Affective Disorders* 136: 310–319.

Barthes, Roland. (1975). "An Introduction to the Structural Analysis of Narrative." Translated by Lionel Duisit. *New Literary History* 6(2): 237–262.

Barthes, Roland. (1977). *Image Music Text*. Translated by Steven Heath. New York: Hill and Wang.

Beauvoir, Simone de. (1980). *The Second Sex*. Translated by H. M. Parshley. New York: Random House.
Beauvoir, Simone de. (2015). *The Ethics of Ambiguity*. Translated by Bernard Frenchtman. New York: Open Road.
Bell, Catherine. (2009). *Ritual Theory, Ritual Practice*. New York: Oxford University Press.
Biebricher, T. (2018). *The Political Theory of Neoliberalism*. Stanford, CA: Stanford University Press.
Bloom, Harold. (1994). *The Western Canon*. New York: Harcourt Brace.
Blum, Jason N. (2012). "Retrieving Phenomenology of Religion as a Method for Religious Studies." *Journal of the American Academy of Religion* 80(4): 1025–1048.
Booth, Wayne C. (1979). *Critical Understanding: The Powers and Limits of Pluralism*. Chicago, IL: The University of Chicago Press.
Bourdieu, Pierre. (1990). *The Logic of Practice*. Stanford, CA: Stanford University Press.
Bourdieu, Pierre. (2000). *Pascalian Meditations*. Stanford, CA: Stanford University Press.
Bruin, John. (2001). *Homo Interrogans: Questioning and the Intentional Structure of Cognition*. Ottawa: University of Ottawa Press.
Buber, Martin. (1970). *I and Thou*. Translated by Walter Kaufmann. New York: Touchstone.
Carlier, J. C. (pseudonym of Cedric Watts). (2000). "Roland Barthes' Resurrection of the Author and Redemption of Biography." *Cambridge Quarterly* 29(4): 386–393.
Cherry, Conrad, Betty A. DeBerg, and Amanda Porterfield. (2001). *Religion on Campus: What Religion Really Means to Today's Undergraduates*. Chapel Hill, NC: University of North Carolina Press.
Cho, Sumi, Kimberlé Williams Crenshaw, and Leslie McCall. (2013). "Toward a Field of Intersectionality Studies: Theory, Application, and Praxis." *Signs* 38(4): 785–810.
Crouch, Margaret A. (2012). "Implicit Bias and Gender (and Other Sorts of) Diversity in Philosophy and the Academy in the Context of the Corporatized University." *Journal of Social Philosophy*, 43(3): 212–226.
Danesi, Marcel. (2016). *The Semiotics of Emoji: The Rise of Visual Language in Age of the Internet*. Bloomsbury Academic.
Davis, Angela. (2005). *Abolition Democracy: Beyond Empire, Prisons, and Torture*. New York: Seven Stories Press.
Davis, Angela. (2016). *Freedom is a Constant Struggle: Ferguson, Palestine, and the Foundations of a Movement*. Chicago, IL: Haymarket Books.
Dawes, Daniel. (2020). *The Political Determinants of Health*. Baltimore, MD: The John Hopkins University Press.

Denny, Mark, and Alan McFadzean. 2011. *Engineering Animals: How Life Works.* Cambridge, MA: Belknap Press.

Derrida, Jacques. (1973). *Speech and Phenomena, and Other Essays on Husserl's Theory of Signs.* Translated by David B. Allison. Evanston, IL: Northwestern University Press.

Derrida, Jacques. (1997). *Of Grammatology.* Translated by Gayatri Chakravorty Spivak. Baltimore, MD: The John Hopkins University Press.

Descartes, René. (1998). *Discourse on Method and Meditations on First Philosophy*, 4th edition. Translated by D. Cress. Indianapolis, IN: Hackett.

DiAngelo, Robin. (2011). "White Fragility." *International Journal of Critical Pedagogy* 3(3): 54–70.

DiAngelo, Robin. (2018). *White Fragility: Why It's So Hard for White People to Talk about Racism.* Boston, MA: Beacon Press.

DiCarlo, Christopher W. (2011). *How to Become a Really Good Pain in the Ass: A Critical Thinker's Guide to Asking the Right Questions.* Amherst, NY: Prometheus Publications.

Dickman, Nathan Eric. (2016). "Linguistically Mediated Liberation: Freedom and Limits of Understanding in Thich Nhat Hanh and Hans-Georg Gadamer." *The Humanistic Psychologist* 44(3): 256–279.

Dickman, Nathan Eric. (2017). "Transcendence Un-Extra-Ordinaire: Bringing the Atheistic I Down to Earth." *Religions* (8)1: 4.

Dickman, Nathan Eric. (2018a). "Hermeneutic Priority and Phenomenological Indeterminacy of Questioning." In *The Significance of Indeterminacy: Perspectives from Asian and Continental Philosophy.* Edited by Robert H. Scott and Gregory S. Moss. New York: Routledge.

Dickman, Nathan Eric. (2018b). "Feminisms and Challenges to Institutionalized Philosophy of Religion." *Religions* 9(4): 113.

Dickman, Nathan Eric. (2020). "Should Religion-Affiliated Institutions Be Accredited? Ricoeur and the Problem of Religious Inclusivity." In Daniel Boscaljon and Jeffrey F. Keuss (eds.), *Paul Ricoeur and the Hope of Higher Education: The Just University.* New York: Lexington Books.

Dickman, Nathan Eric. (2021a). *Using Questions to Think: How to Develop Skills in Critical Understanding and Reasoning.* New York: Bloomsbury.

Dickman, Nathan Eric. (2021b). "The Hermeneutic Priority of Which Question? A Speech Act Clarification for Interlocutionary Acts." *Informal Logic* 41(3): 485–508.

Dickman, Nathan Eric. (2021c). "Where, Not When, Did the Cosmos 'Begin'?" *Sophia* 60: 67–81.

Dickman, Nathan Eric. (2022a). *Philosophical Hermeneutics and the Priority of Questions in Religions: Bringing the Discourse of Gods and Buddhas Down to Earth.* New York: Bloomsbury.

Dickman, Nathan Eric. (2022b). "Radical Responsibility beyond Empathy: Interreligious Resources against (Neo)Liberal Distortions of Nursing Care." *Nursing Philosophy* 23(1): e12372.

Dickman, Nathan Eric. (2022c). "Physical Distance, Ethical Proximity: Levinasian Dialogue as Pandemic Pedagogy in Faceless (Masked or Online) Classrooms." *Teaching Philosophy* 44(3): 255–279.

Dilthey, Wilhelm. (1972). "The Rise of Hermeneutics." Translated by Fredric Jameson. *New Literary History* 3(2): 229–244.

Dilthey, Wilhelm. (1988). *Introduction to the Human Sciences: An Attempt to Lay a Foundation for the Study of Society and History*. Translated by R. Betanzos. Detroit, MI: Wayne State University Press.

Dupre, Louis. (1993). *Passage to Modernity: An Essay in the Hermeneutics of Nature and Culture*. New Haven, CT: Yale University Press.

Edelglass, William, and Jay Garfield (eds.). (2009). *Buddhist Philosophy: Essential Readings*. Oxford: Oxford University Press.

Everett, Daniel L. (2017). *How Language Began: The Story of Humanity's Greatest Invention*. New York: Liveright Publishing.

Fackenheim, Emil. (1986). "Concerning Authentic and Inauthentic Responses to the Holocaust." *Holocaust and Genocide Studies* 1(1): 101–120.

Fanon, Frantz. (2008). *Black Skin White Masks*. Translated by Charles Lam Markmann. London: Plato Press.

Faure, Bernard. (2009). *Unmasking Buddhism*. Oxford: Wiley-Blackwell.

Feuerbach, Ludwig. (1989). *The Essence of Christianity*. Translated by George Eliot. Amherst, MA: Prometheus Books.

Fish, Stanley. (1980). *Is There a Text in this Class? The Authority of Interpretive Communities*. Cambridge, MA: Harvard University Press.

Fish, Stanley. (2010). "The Crisis of the Humanities Officially Arrives." *The New York Times*, October 11.

Foucault, Michel. (1983). *Michel Foucault: Beyond Structuralism and Hermeneutics*, 2nd edition. Edited by Hubert L. Dreyfus and Paul Rabinow. Chicago, IL: The University of Chicago Press.

Foucault, Michel. (1998). *Aesthetics, Method, and Epistemology*, vol. II. Translated by Robert Hurley. New York: The New Press.

Foucault, Michel. (2002). *The Order of Things: An Archeology of the Human Sciences*. London: Routledge Classics.

Freire, Paulo. (2001). *Pedagogy of Freedom: Ethics, Democracy, and Civic Courage*. Translated by Patrick Clarke. Lanham, MD: Rowan and Littlefield Publishers.

Friedlander, Saul. (2001). "The Shoah in Present Historical Consciousness." In Michael L. Morgan (ed.), *A Holocaust Reader: Responses to the Nazi Extermination*. Oxford: Oxford University Press.

Frotrell, Q. (2020). "Trump Calls Dr. Fauci a 'Disaster'—Fauci Tells Americans: 'Stay Away from the Politics.'" *Market Watch*, October 20. Retrieved from www.marketwatch.com/story/when-making-decisions-about-covid-19-dr-fauci-says-stay-away-from-the-politics-2020-10-19.

Gadamer, Hans-Georg. (1977). *Philosophical Hermeneutics*. Translated and edited by David E. Linge. Berkeley, CA: University of California Press.

Gadamer, Hans-Georg. (1980). "The Eminent Text and Its Truth." *The Bulletin of the Midwest Modern Language Association* 13(1): 3–10.

Gadamer, Hans-Georg. (1986). *The Idea of the Good in Platonic-Aristotelian Philosophy*. Translated by P. Christopher Smith. New Haven, CT: Yale University Press.

Gadamer, Hans-Georg. (1989). "Text and Interpretation." Translated by D. Schmidt and R. Palmer. In D. Michelfelder and R. Palmer (eds.), *Dialogue and Deconstruction: The Gadamer-Derrida Encounter*, pp. 21–51. Albany, NY: SUNY Press.

Gadamer, Hans-Georg. (2007). *The Gadamer Reader: A Bouquet of the Later Writings*. Edited by Richard E. Palmer. Evanston, IL: Northwestern University Press.

Gadamer, Hans-Georg. (2013). *Truth and Method*, 2nd revised edition. Translated by Joel Weinsheimer and Donald G. Marshall. London: Bloomsbury Academic.

Gawande, Atul. (2017). *Being Mortal: Medicine and What Matters in the End*. New York: Picador.

Gillon, Brendan S. (2013). "Language and Logic in Indian Buddhist Thought." In S. Emmanuel (ed.), *A Companion to Buddhist Philosophy*, pp. 307–319. Chichester: Wiley-Blackwell.

Gould, Rebecca. (2014). "The Poetics from Athens to al Andalus: Ibn Rushd's Grounds for Comparison." *Modern Philology* 112(1): 1–24.

Graff, Harvey J. (2010). "The Literacy Myth at Thirty." *Journal of Social History* 43(3): 635–661.

Grondin, Jean. (1994). *Introduction to Philosophical Hermeneutics*. Translated by Joel Weinsheimer. New Haven, CT: Yale University Press.

Gummer, Natalie. (2020). The Scandal of the Speaking Buddha: Performative Utterance and the Erotics of the Dharma." In Rafal K. Stepien (ed.), *Buddhist Literature as Philosophy, Buddhist Philosophy as Literature*, pp. 197–239. Albany, NY: SUNY Press.

Haidu, Peter. (1992). "The Dialectics of Unspeakability: Language, Silence, and the Narratives of Desubjectification." In Saul Friedlander (ed.), *Probing the Limits of Representation: Nazism and the "Final Solution."* Cambridge, MA: Harvard University Press.

Hall, Stuart. (1990). "The Emergence of Cultural Studies and the Crisis of the Humanities." *October* 53: 11–23.

Harper, Sandra S. (2015). "Drawing Out." In *Conversations: Leading United Methodist-related Schools, Colleges, and Universities*. Edited by M. Kathryn Armistead and Melanie B. Overton. The United Methodist Church: General Board of Higher Education and Ministry.

Harpham, Geoffrey Galt. (2009). "The Humanities' Value." *Chronicle of Higher Education* 55(28): B6.

Harvey, Peter. (2009). "Theravada Philosophy of Mind." In *Buddhist Philosophy: Essential Readings*. Edited by William Edelglass and Jay L. Garfield. New York: Oxford University Press.

Hegel, Georg Wilhelm Friedrich. (1977). *The Phenomenology of Spirit*. Translated by A.V. Miller. Oxford: Oxford University Press.

Hegel, Georg Wilhelm Friedrich. (1997). *On Art, Religion, and the History of Philosophy: Introductory Lectures*. Edited by J. Glenn Gray. Indianapolis, IN: Hackett Publishing.

Heidegger, Martin. (2001). "The Origin of the Work of Art." In Martin Heidegger, *Poetry, Language, Thought*. Translated by Albert Hofstadter. New York: HarperCollins.

Herbjørnsrud, Dag. (2017). "The African Enlightenment." *AEON*, December.

Hintikka, Jakko. (2000). *On Wittgenstein*. Belmont, CA: Wadsworth.

Hirsch, E. D. (1967). *Validity in Interpretation*. New Haven, CT: Yale University Press.

Hollywood, Amy. (1998). "Deconstructing Belief: Irigaray and the Philosophy of Religion." *The Journal of Religion* 78(2): 230–245.

Hughes, Aaron W., and Russell T. McCutcheon. (2022). *Religion in 50 Words: A Critical Vocabulary*. New York: Routledge.

Husserl, Edmund. (1973). *Experience and Judgment: Investigations in a Genealogy of Logic*. Translated by James S. Churchill and Karl Ameriks. Evanston, IL: Northwestern University Press.

Husserl, Edmund. (1990). *The Idea of Phenomenology*. Translated by William P. Alston and Georga Nakhnikian. Dordrecht: Kluwer Academic Publishers.

Irigaray, Luce. (2002). *The Way of Love*. Translated by Heidi Bostic and Stephen Pluhacek. London: Bloomsbury.

Irigaray, Luce. (2007). *Je, Tu, Nous: Toward a Culture of Difference*. Translated by Alison Martin. London: Routledge Classics.

Iser, Wolfgang. (1972). "The Reading Process: A Phenomenological Approach." *New Literary History* 3(2): 279–299.

Iser, Wolfgang. (1975). "The Reality of Fiction: A Functionalist Approach to Literature." *New Literary History* 7(1): 7–38.

Kafer, Allison. (2013). *Feminist, Queer, Crip*. Bloomington, IN: Indiana University Press.

Kant, Immanuel. (2007). *Critique of Pure Reason.* Translated by Marcus Weigelt. London: Penguin Classics.

Katz, Jonathan Ned. (1995). *The Invention of Heterosexuality.* Chicago, IL: The University of Chicago Press.

Kendi, Ibram X. (2019). *How To Be an Antiracist.* New York: OneWorld.

Khazanchi, R., C. Evans, and J. Marcelin. (2020). "Racism, Not Race, Drives Inequity across the COVID-19 Continuum." *Journal of the American Medical Association: Network Open* 3(9): e2019933.

Klemm, David E. (2008). "Philosophy and Kerygma: Ricoeur as Reader of the Bible." In D. Kaplan (ed.), *Reading Ricoeur,* pp. 47–70. Albany, NY: SUNY Press.

Klemm, David E., and William Schweiker. (2008). *Religion and the Human Future: An Essay on Theological Humanism.* Malden, MA: Wiley Blackwell.

Knepper, Timothy. (2013). *The Ends of Philosophy of Religion: Terminus and Telos.* New York: Palgrave Macmillan.

Kwok, Pui-lan. (2016). "Reading the Christian New Testament in the Contemporary World." In Margaret Aymer et al. (eds.), *The Gospels and Acts: Fortress Commentary on the Bible Study Edition,* pp. 5–30. Minneapolis, MN: Augsburg Fortress Publishers.

Lang, Berel (ed.). (1988). *Writing and the Holocaust.* New York: Holmes and Meier.

Latvus, Kari. (2006). "Decolonizing Yahweh: A Postcolonial Reading of 2 Kings 24–25." In Rasiah S. Sugirtharajah (ed.), *Voices from the Margin: Interpreting the Bible in the Third World,* 3rd edition, pp. 186–192. Maryknoll, NY: Orbis Books.

Lee, Emily. (2014). "Bodily Movement and Responsibility for a Situation." In E. Lee (ed.), *Living Alterities: Phenomenology, Embodiment, and Race.* Albany, NY: SUNY Press.

Levinas, Emmanuel. (1998). *Entre Nous: On Thinking-of-the-Other.* Translated by Michael Bradshaw. New York: Columbia University Press.

Levine, Amy-Jill. (2015). *Short Stories by Jesus: The Enigmatic Parables of a Controversial Rabbi.* New York: HaperOne.

Lewis, Thomas. (2016). *Why Philosophy Matters for the Study of Religion—and Vice Versa.* Oxford: Oxford University Press.

Loy, David. (2013). "The Lack of Self: A Western Buddhist Psychology." In R. Jackson and J. Makransky (eds.), *Buddhist Theology: Critical Reflections by Contemporary Buddhist Scholars,* pp. 155–172. New York: Routledge.

MacIntyre, Alasdair. (1981). *After Virtue.* Notre Dame, IN: University of Notre Dame Press.

Mandel, Naomi. (2001). "Rethinking 'After Auschwitz': Against a Rhetoric of the Unspeakable in Holocaust Writing." *boundary* 2.28(2): 203–228.

Manne, Kate. (2020). *Entitled: How Male Privilege Hurts Women*. New York: Crown Publishing.

Martin, Bill, Jr., and Eric Carle. (1967). *Brown Bear, Brown Bear, What Do You See?* New York: Harcourt Brace and Company.

Masuzawa, Tomoko. (2005). *The Invention of World Religions*. Chicago, IL: The University of Chicago Press.

Matsumoto Shirō. (1997). "The Doctrine of Tathagata-Garbha Is Not Buddhist." Translated by Jamie Hubbard. In Jamie Hubbard (ed.), *Pruning the Bodhi Tree: The Storm Over Critical Buddhism*. Honolulu, HI: University of Hawaii Press.

Matusov, Eugene, and John St. Julien. (2004). "Print Literacy as Oppression: Cases of Bureaucratic, Colonial, and Totalitarian Literacies and the Implications for Schooling." *Texts* 24(2): 197–244.

Mbembe, Achille. (2017). *Critique of Black Reason*. Translated by Laurent Bubois. Durham: Duke University Press.

McCutcheon, Russell T. (1997). *Manufacturing Religion: The Discourse on Sui Generis Religion and the Politics of Nostalgia*. New York: Oxford University Press.

McGary, Howard. (2003). "Alienation and the African-American Experience." In P. H. Coetzee and A. P. J. Roux (eds.), *The African Philosophy Reader*, 2nd edition, pp. 688–700. New York: Routledge.

McIntosh, Kathleen, and Kate Bagley. (2007). *Women's Studies in Religion: A Multicultural Reader*. New York: Pearson.

McKenzie, Steven L., and Stephen R. Haynes. (1999). *To Each Its Own Meaning: An Introduction to Biblical Criticism*. Louisville, KY: Westminster John Knox Press.

McRae, John R. (2003). *Seeing Through Zen: Encounter, Transformation, and Genealogy in Chinese Chan Buddhism*. Berkeley, CA: University of California Press.

Merleau-Ponty, Maurice. (1968). *The Visible and the Invisible*. Translated by A. Lingis. Evanston, IL: Northwestern University Press.

Merleau-Ponty, Maurice. (2002). *Phenomenology of Perception*. Translated by C. Smith. New York: Routledge.

Meyer, Michel. (1995). *Of Problematology: Philosophy, Science, and Language*. Translated by D. Jamison. Chicago, IL: The University of Chicago Press.

Moyaert, Marianne. (2010). "Absorption or Hospitality: Two Approaches to the Tension between Identity and Alterity." *Interreligious Hermeneutics*. Edited by C. Cornille and C. Conway. Eugene, OR: Cascade Books.

Mueller-Vollmer, Kurt. (2000). *The Hermeneutics Reader: Texts of the German Tradition from the Enlightenment to the Present*. New York: Continuum.

Müller, Max. (1873). *Introduction to the Science of Religion*. London: Longman, Green, and Co.

Nagarjuna. (1995). *The Fundamental Wisdom of the Middle Way*. Translated by Jay L Garfield. Oxford: Oxford University Press.
Newfield, Christopher. (2009). "Ending the Budget Wars: Funding the Humanities during a Crisis in Higher Education." *Profession* 2009(1): 270–284.
Nietzsche, Friedrich. (2008). *On the Genealogy of Morals*. Translated by Douglas Smith. Oxford: Oxford University Press.
Nussbaum, Martha C. (1995). "Objectification." *Philosophy and Public Affairs* 24(4): 249–291.
Okun, Tema. (2001). *White Supremacy Culture*. dRworks (Dismantling Racism Works). Retrieved from www.whitesupremacyculture.info/.
Oluo, Ijeoma. (2019). *So You Want to Talk about Race?* New York: Seal Press.
Oluo, Ijeoma. (2020). *Mediocre: The Dangerous Legacy of White Male America*. New York: Seal Press.
Pan, David. (1998). "The Crisis of the Humanities and the End of the University." *Telos* 111: 69–106.
Parkes, Graham. (2009). "Dogen's 'Mountains and Waters as Sutras' (Sansuikyo)." In W. Edelglass and J. Garfield (eds.), *Buddhist Philosophy: Essential Readings*, pp. 83–92. Oxford: Oxford University Press.
Plato. (1991). *The Republic*, 2nd edition. Translated by Alan Bloom. New York: Basic Books.
Plummer, Robert. (2010). *40 Questions about the Bible*. Grand Rapids, MI: Kregel.
Prothero, Stephen. (2008). *Religious Literacy: What Every American Needs to Know—And Doesn't*. San Francisco, CA: HarperOne.
Raphael, Taffy E. (1986). "Teaching Question Answer Relationships, Revisited." *The Reading Teacher* 39(6): 516–522.
Ricoeur, Paul. (1974). "Philosophy of Religious Language." *The Journal of Religion* 54(1): 71–85.
Ricoeur, Paul. (1975). "Phenomenology and Hermeneutics." *Noûs* 9(1): 85–102.
Ricoeur, Paul. (1976). *Interpretation Theory: Discourse and the Surplus of Meaning*. Fort Worth, TX: Texas Christian University Press.
Ricoeur, Paul. (1986). "Life: A Story in Search of a Narrator." Translated by Marinus C. Doeser and John N. Kraay (eds.), *Facts and Values: Philosophical Reflections from Western and Non-Western Perspectives*. Dordrecht: Martinus Nijhoff Publishers.
Ricoeur, Paul. (1988). *Time and Narrative*, vol. III. Translated by Kathleen Blamey and David Pellauer. Chicago, IL: The University of Chicago Press.
Ricoeur, Paul. (1991). "Hermeneutics and the Critique of Ideology." Translated by K. Blamey and J. Thompson. In Paul Ricoeur, *From Text to Action: Essays in Hermeneutics*, II. Northwestern University Press.

Ricoeur, Paul. (1995). *Figuring the Sacred: Religion, Narrative, and Imagination*. Translated by David Pellauer. Minneapolis, MN: Fortress Press.

Ricoeur, Paul. (1998). "Violence and Language." *Journal of French and Francophone Philosophy* 10(2): 32–41.

Ricoeur, Paul. (2003). *The Rule of Metaphor*. Translated by Robert Czerny. London: Routledge Classics.

Ricoeur, Paul. (2010). "Religious Belief: The Difficult Path of the Religious." In Brain Treanor and Henry Isaac Venema (eds.), *A Passion for the Possible: Thinking with Paul Ricoeur*, pp. 27–40. New York: Fordham University Press.

Ronkin, Noah. (2009). "Theravada Metaphysics and Ontology." In W. Edelglass and J. Garfield (eds.), *Buddhist Philosophy: Essential Readings*, pp. 13–26. New York: Oxford University Press.

Rorty, Richard. (2004). "Being That Can Be Understood Is Language." In Bruce Krajewski (ed.), *Gadamer's Repercussions: Reconsidering Philosophical Hermeneutics*, pp. 21–29. Berkeley, CA: University of California Press.

Rothman, Jason. (2008). "Linguistic Epistemology and the Notion of Monoligualism." *Sociolinguistic Studies* 2(3): 441–457.

Said, Edward. (1997). *Covering Islam: How the Media and the Experts Determine How We See the Rest of the World*, revised edition. New York: Vintage Press.

Sartre, Jean-Paul. (1991). *The Transcendence of the Ego: An Existentialist Theory of Consciousness*. Translated by Forrest Williams and Robert Kirkpatrick. New York: Hill and Wang.

Sartre, Jean-Paul. (1993). *Being and Nothingness*. Translated by Hazel E. Barnes. New York: Washington Square Press.

Scharlemann, Robert P. (1981). *The Being of God: Theology and the Experience of Truth*. New York: Seabury Press.

Schilbrack, Kevin. (2014). *Philosophy and the Study of Religions: A Manifesto*. Malden, MA: Wiley Blackwell.

Schleiermacher, Friedrich. (1977). *Hermeneutics: The Handwritten Manuscripts*. Edited by Heinz Kimmerle. Translated by James Duke and Jack Forstman. Missoula, MT: Scholars Press.

Schleiermacher, Friedrich. (1978). "The Hermeneutics: Outline of the 1819 Lectures." Translated by Jan Wojcik and Roland Hass. *New Literary History* 10(1): 1–16.

Schmidt, Lawrence K. (2006). *Understanding Hermeneutics*. Stocksfield: Acumen Publishing.

Schuhmann, Karl, and Barry Smith. (1987). "Questions: An Essay in Daubertian Phenomenology." *Philosophy and Phenomenological Research* 47(3): 353–384.

Segal, Robert A. (2014). "Interpretation and Explanation: A Response to Jason Blum's Defense of Phenomenology of Religion." *Journal of the American Academy of Religion* 82(4): 1149–1151.

Sells, Michael. (2007). *Approaching the Qur'an: The Early Revelations*, 2nd edition. Ashland, OR: White Cloud Press.

Sharf, Robert H. (1995). "Buddhist Modernism and the Rhetoric of Meditative Experience." *Numen* 42(3): 228–283.

Skloot, R. (2011). *The Immortal Life of Henrietta Lacks*. New York: Broadway Books.

Smith, Mitzi J. (2017). *Insights from African American Interpretation*. Minneapolis, MN: Fortress Press.

Smyth, Joshua M., Jill R. Hockemeyer, and Heather Tulloch. (2008). "Expressive Writing and Post-Traumatic Stress Disorder: Effects on Trauma Symptoms, Mood States, and Cortisol Reactivity." *Health Psychology* 13(1): 85–93.

Srinivasan, Amia. (2021). *The Right to Sex: Feminism in the Twenty-First Century*. New York: Farrar, Straus and Giroux.

St. Clair, Raquel A. (2007). "Womanist Biblical Interpretation." In Brian K. Blount et al. (eds.), *True to Our Native Land: An African American New Testament Commentary*. Minneapolis, MN: Fortress Press.

St. Clair, Raquel A. (2008). *Call and Consequences: A Womanist Reading of Mark*. Minneapolis, MN: Fortress Press.

Stout, Jeffrey. (2005). *Democracy and Tradition*. Princeton, NJ: Princeton University Press.

Strong, John R. (2002). *The Experience of Buddhism: Sources and Interpretations*, 2nd edition. Belmont: Wadsworth.

Taylor, Charles. (1985). *Philosophical Papers, Vol. 1: Human Agency and Language*. Cambridge: Cambridge University Press.

Taylor, Charles. (1989). *Sources of the Self: The Making of Modern Identity*. Cambridge, MA: Harvard University Press.

Theunissen, Michael. (1984). *The Other: Studies in the Social Ontology of Husserl, Heidegger, Sartre, and Buber*. Translated by Christopher Macann. Cambridge, MA: MIT Press.

Thiem, Annika. (2014). "The Art of Queer Rejections: The Everyday Life of Biblical Discourse." *Neotestamentica* 48(1): 33–56.

Tillich, Paul. (2001). *Dynamics of Faith*. New York: HarperCollins.

Urciuoli, Bonnie. (2011). "Semiotic Properties of Racializing Discourses." *Journal of Linguistic Anthropology* 21(1): 113–122.

Vanhoozer, Kevin J. (1998). *Is There a Meaning in This Text? The Bible, the Reader, and The Morality of Literary Knowledge*. Grand Rapids, MI: Zondervan.

Vayntrub, Jacqueline. (2019). *Beyond Orality: Biblical Poetry on Its Own Terms*. New York: Routledge.

Warnke, Georgia. (1997). "Legitimate Prejudices." *Laval theologique et philosophique* 53(1): 89–102.
Weiss, Gail. (2008). *Refiguring the Ordinary*. Bloomington, IN: Indiana University Press.
Weldon, S. Laurel. (2015). "Intersectionality." In Gary Goertz and Amy G. Mazur (eds.), *Politics, Gender, and Concepts: Theory and Methodology*. New York: Cambridge University Press.
Welton, Donn. (1999). *The Essential Husserl: Basic Writings in Transcendental Phenomenology*. Bloomington, IN: Indiana University Press.
Williams, Kevin. (2021). "Voices of the Establishment or of Cultural Subversion? The Western Canon in the Curriculum." *Journal of Philosophy of Education*. 55: 864–877.
Wiredu, Kwasi. (1997). "How Not to Compare African Traditional Thought with Western Thought." *Transitions* 75/76: 320–327.
Wittgenstein, Ludwig. (1965). "A Lecture on Ethics." *The Philosophical Review* 74(1): 3–12.
Wittgenstein, Ludwig. (1999). *Tractatus Logico-Philosophicus*. Translated by C. K. Ogden. Mineola, NY: Dover.
Wittgenstein, Ludwig. (2009). *Philosophical Investigations*, revised 4th edition. Translated by G. E. M. Amscombe, P. M. S. Hacker, and Joachim Schulte. New York: Wiley-Blackwell.
Wolfart, Johannes C. (2022). "'Religious Literacy' Some Considerations and Reservations." *Method and Theory in the Study of Religion*. Online ahead of print.
Wolterstorff, Nicolas. (1995). *Divine Discourse: Philosophical Reflections on the Claim that God Speaks*. New York: Cambridge University Press.
Wolterstorff, Nicholas. (2006). "Resuscitating the Author." In Kevin J. Vanhoozer, James K. A. Smith, and Bruce Ellis Benson (eds.), *Hermeneutics at the Crossroads*, pp. 35–50. Bloomington, IN: Indiana University Press.
Wright, Dale S. (2003). "Empty Texts/Sacred Meaning: Reading as Spiritual Practice in Chinese Buddhism." *Dao: A Journal of Comparative Philosophy* 11(2): 261–272.
X, Malcolm. (1992). *The Autobiography of Malcolm X, as told to Alex Haley*. New York. Ballantine Books.
Yancy, George. (2000). "The Black Self within a Semiotic Space of Whiteness: Reflections on the Racial Deformation of Pecola Breedlove in Toni Morrison's 'The Bluest Eye.'" *CLA Journal* 43(3): 299–319.
Zigon, Jarrett. (2018). *Disappointment: Toward a Critical Hermeneutics of Worldbuilding*. New York: Fordham University Press.

Index

ableism 10, 53, 54, 60
Adorno, Theodor 37, 69
allusions 9, 23
anachronism 115, 127–128
anatman 55
Anderson, Pamela Sue 44
animal tracks 3
Anselm 29
anti-vax movement 38
antithesis-centered questioning 87–88
application 113, 116–117
appropriation 100, 112, 120–122
Aristotle 3, 32
art 10, 17, 81–82, 83
Asad, Talal 68, 70
Aslan, Reza 5
assertions 50, 58, 59, 85
atheists 131–132
Auschwitz 69, 70
authorial discourse interpretation 22
authority 5, 6, 22, 29, 58, 63, 123
authors/authorship 22, 95, 115
autostereograms 82, 92, 95, 103, 136

Babel 65
Bachelor of Science (BS) degrees 37
Bacon, Francis 60
Bagley, Kate 107
Barthes, Roland 26, 95, 99
Beauvoir, Simone de 44, 53, 54, 59–60, 79
Bedeutung 15
behind-the-lines questions 103, 114
Bell, Catherine 124, 125, 126

between-the-lines questions 102, 105, 114
beyond-the-lines questions 103–104, 105, 116
Bhagavad Gita 101–102
bias 4, 6, 43, 56
Bible 2, 22, 24–25, 65, 102, 127, 128
  see also New Testament
bodily dehiscence 84–85
books 2, 29
  etymology of 7
  as non-interpretable 93
  otherness of 100
  popup 92, 95
  as semantic fields 92–93
  and texts, compared *see under* texts
brackets *see epoche*
Braille 3, 7, 33
BS (Bachelor of Science) degrees 37
Buber, Martin 9–10
Buddha 55, 110, 127
Buddhism 2, 4, 28, 36, 61, 100, 128
  academic study of 130
  Chan 108, 122
  and emptiness 55–56, 75
  institutions of 108
  and language 75
  Madhyamaka Buddhism 55–56
  and self/soul 55
  Theravadin 9, 130
business schools 36, 37

Campbell, Joseph 83
capitalism 25, 36, 37, 39, 42, 45, 81

Chan Buddhism 108, 122
childhood literacy pedagogy 101, 102, 104–105
Christianity 4, 5, 28, 36, 100–101, 103, 110
   and homosexuality 115
   and limits of language 69
   and philosophy of religion 130
   Reformation 43, 123
   and religious literacy 131
   and supremicism 60–61
   see also Bible; New Testament
classic texts 91, 105–111
   and imitation/originality 110
   as listeners 106–107
   and questions 110–111
   re-reading 106, 107
   as timeless 106
   and traditions 107–110
Clinton, George 21
colonialism 17, 43, 45, 60, 132
   see also Eurocentrism
community of readers 24, 29
complete thoughts 13, 14, 15, 16, 17, 50, 57, 67
   and appropriation 120–121
   and meaning/understanding 70, 72, 85, 89, 120
   and predicates 80
   and propositions 75
   and questions 31, 33, 86, 92, 104
   and reading aloud 95
   texts as 112
comprehension 18, 91, 113, 115–116
concatenation 15, 94
conclusion-centered questioning 87, 104
conjecture 113–114
consciousness 11, 17, 45–46, 48–50, 79, 84
   interpretive *see* interpretive consciousness
   noetic/noematic poles of 49, 54, 57
   pure 48

context 1, 9, 15, 21, 53, 55, 79, 116, 128
   historical 17, 103, 114, 119
   personal/social 2, 27, 124
   and prejudice 57–58
   and questions 33, 103, 110
   religious 4–5, 132
   and self-expression 22
   and social practices 124
conversation *see* dialogue
copula 13, 49, 50, 58, 86–87
correctness of interpretations 16, 19–20
   and hermeneutic fallacies *see* hermeneutic fallacies
   and logical fallacies 27–28
   and questions *see* questions
   and reader *see* reader, and correctness of interpretation
   and text 19, 20, 25–26, 27, 29
   and writer *see* writer, and correctness of interpretation
COVID-19 pandemic 38
Crip Theory 18
Critical Race Theory 18, 39
critical thinking 19
cultural traditions *see* traditions

dance 6
Daubert, Johannes 86
Davis, Angela 39, 127
Dawkins, Richard 131–132
death of the author 26–27
dehiscence, bodily 84–85
dependent emergence 55–56
Derrida, Jacques 12, 54, 92–93, 121
Descartes, Rene 43–44, 45, 60
Dharmakirti 75
dialectic-centered questioning 88
dialogue 3–4, 17, 63–64, 66, 67, 73–78, 90, 96, 112
   and language systems 73–74
   and meaning/understanding 71–72, 76
   and questions 87–88
   and reading 96, 97, 104

and responsibility 121
rules of 76–77
and shared environment 98
and signs 74–76
as social practice 124
and text 78, 97–98, 100, 104, 107, 111, 115–116, 119
and transcendental subjectivity 64, 89
writer–reader 97
dictionaries 14, 73–74
Dignaga 75
Dilthey, Wilhelm 21, 22
discourse 3, 7, 14, 29, 45–46, 50, 134–135
  appropriation 22–23
  and appropriation 120–121
  and dialogue 76
  and predication 83–84
  questions in *see* questions
  and rhetoric 42
  rules of 76–77, 83, 89
  and texts 91
dualism, metaphysical 44
Dunning-Kruger effect 63

ecocriticism 127
effluvia model 84–85
ego 48, 51–52, 55
eidetic reduction 50–51
eidetic universals 50, 51
embodiment 44–45, 81, 84, 85
emojis/emoticons 9, 12
emotivism 39
empathy 21, 71, 72, 77, 135
emptiness 55–56, 75
Enlightenment 6
epoche 47–48, 49–50, 52
erotetic logic 35
essentialism 50–51
Eurocentrism 17, 36, 43, 45, 59–64, 112, 126
  and classic texts 105–106, 127
  and hierarchy of religions 60–61
  and liberalism 62
  and meritocracy 63
  and presumption of neutrality 43, 62
exclusion 44, 75
exegesis/eisegesis 5–6
exegetical/existential hermeneutic circle 118–119
expertise, suspicion of 38
explanation 113, 114–115
externalization 22, 80–81

Facebook 7
Fackenheim, Emil 69, 70
Fanon, Franz 53–54, 60
fascism 38, 39
Fauci, Anthony 38
feminism 18, 45, 53, 115
Fish, Stanley 5, 24, 26–27, 105, 128
fitness industry 125
Foucault, Michel 52, 72, 125
freedom 40, 42, 106, 122
  and rules/constraints 73, 80, 83, 103, 104, 129
Freire, Paulo 134, 135
Freud, Sigmund 54
Friedlander, Saul 69
friendship 4, 32

Gadamer, Hans-Georg 39–40, 46–47, 52, 92
  and application 116–117
  and classic texts 106
  and dialogue 76, 77
  and language 65–66
  and meaning of text 25, 30, 31, 34
  and prejudice 47, 59, 60, 63
  and questioning 40, 98, 122
  and traditions 99–100, 109, 110, 124
  and understanding 70, 71
games/play 76, 77–78, 92
Genesis 102
genres 94, 127
Graff, Harvey J. 132
grammar 13, 71–72, 74, 84

Grondin, Jean 123
'Guernica' (Picasso) 69

Hadiths 4
Haidu, Peter 69
Harper, Sandra S. 40
HaShem 24, 65, 69
health care 62, 108
Hegel, Georg Wilhelm Friedrich 80–81, 122
hegemonies
    of Eurocentrism 36, 62, 105
    of ideologies 61
    of neoliberalism 41
    redemptive 125–126
    white 63
hermeneutic fallacies 27, 28–30
    fallacy of the absolute text 28–29
    fallacy of reader caprice 29
    intentional fallacy 28
hermeneutical arc/circle/coil 117–119, 128, 133
hermeneutics 15–16, 17, 19, 20–22, 133–134
    double 22
    and phenomenology 54
    and psychology 28, 30
    and questions *see* questions
    and rhetoric 42
    romantic 21–22
    and validation 21
    of wholeness 25
heteronormativity 127
hierarchies 60–61, 124
higher education institutions 37, 38, 41
Hindutva movement 4–5
Hintikka, Jakko 103
Hirsch, E.D. 21
Holocaust *see* Shoah
homosexuality 115
human rights 45
humanism 43
humanities 17, 19, 36–41
    and use-value 36–37

Husserl, Edmund 17, 43, 47–48, 49, 50–52, 54, 84
hypertext 9
hypothesis 21

ideology 23, 24–25, 61, 63
imagination 49, 50
imperialism 45
individualism 39–40, 42, 109, 114, 122, 124
inference-centered questioning 87
institutional model 23, 24
institutions 37–38, 39, 107–108, 123, 124
    and power 29, 58, 106, 124–125
    and prejudice 62
intentional fallacy 28
intentionality 43, 47, 48, 49, 84, 121
Internet 9
interpretation
    and complexity 1
    correct/incorrect *see* correctness of interpretations
    four steps for 112, 113–117
    and literality/amplification 4–5
    pluralities of 127–128
    product/process of 112, 117–120
    social/institutional aspects of 18
    ubiquity of 1, 2–6
interpretive communities 112–113, 126–128
interpretive consciousness 42, 46–59, 112
    and dependent emergence 55–56
    and discourse 50
    and eidetic reduction 50–51
    and *epoche* 47–48, 49–50, 52
    and history 53–59
    and noetic/noematic moments 49, 57
    and prejudice 56–59
    and pure consciousness 48
    and transcendental reduction 51–53

and transcendental subjectivity 52–53, 54–55
intersubjectivity 10, 53
Irigaray, Luce 44–45, 59–60, 85, 96, 125
Iser, Wolfgang 23–24
Islam/Muslims 4, 36, 60, 61, 63, 80, 131, 132
and rules 73
I-It/I-Thou modes of existence 9–10

Jakata Tales 127
Jesus 100, 103, 105, 110
John 105
Jonah, Book of 24
Judaism 36, 103, 119, 131

Kaepernick, Colin 61
Kant, Immanuel 46, 48, 66–67
Klemm, David 26
knowledge 22, 66–67, 88
　Eurocentric 61, 62, 63
　objective 44, 50, 51
Kwok Pui-Lan 61–62, 127

Lacks, Henrietta 38
Lang, Berel 69
language 3, 6, 7, 11, 17, 50, 64, 67–84
　and dictionaries 14, 73–74
　limits of *see* limits of language
　occularcentrism of 54
　and polylingualism 78
　and responsibility 121
　and semantics 13–15
　and signs *see* signs
　systems 17, 67, 73, 74, 78
　and translation 65–66
　universal 65
　see also dialogue; discourse
Latvus, Kari 24
leisure 37, 40
Levinas, Emmanuel 88, 121
Levine, Amy-Jill 103
Lewis, Thomas A. 131, 132
liberal arts 39, 40
liberalism 38, 39, 43, 62

limits of language 67–71
　and Holocaust 69
　and meaning 70–71
literacy 34, 101, 102, 104–105, 132
　see also religious literacy
literary canons 17
literary criticism 5, 36, 115
Locke, John 45
logical fallacies 27–28
logon 3
Lord of the Rings trilogy (Tolkien) 102
Luke 22, 105
Luther, Martin 123

McGary, Howard 62
MacIntosh, Kathleen 107
MacIntyre, Alasdair 76
Madhyamaka Buddhism 55–56
Magic 8 Ball method 38, 123
"Magic Eye" pictures (autostereograms) 82, 92, 95, 136
Malcolm X 122
Mandel, Naomi 69, 70
Manne, Kate 62
marginalization 53–54, 62
Mark 105
Marx, Karl/Marxism 12, 54
Masuzawa, Tomoko 60
Matthew 105
Mbembe, Achille 45, 59–60, 81–82
meaning 16, 33–34, 50, 70–71, 119–122
　and appropriation 120–122
　and discourse 71–72
　and Holocaust 69, 70
　and predicates 82–83
　and suicide bombings 68, 70
　and understanding 33
media 63
memory 49
meritocracy 63
Merleau-Ponty, Maurice 84–85
metaphor 80
metaphysics 44, 51, 52, 55, 118
#MeToo movement 37

Meyer, Michel 75
mind-body problem 44
Modus Ponens 27
Moyaert, Marianne 66
Müller, Max 78
music 21, 77, 92, 116, 119
   see also songs
Muslims *see* Islam/Muslims

Nagarjuna 44, 55–56, 87
neoliberalism 36–37, 81, 113
   and individualism/freedom 39, 40, 42, 109, 114, 122
   and questioning 40–41
   and racism 45
   and "rights" discourse 127
   and science 37, 39, 40
neutrality, presumption of 43, 44, 60, 61, 62
New Testament 2, 22, 25, 105, 128
Nietzsche, Friedrich 54, 66
noetic/noematic moments 49, 54, 57

objectification 10, 13, 43, 116
occularcentrism 54
Oluo, Ijeoma 63
on-the-lines questions 101–102, 105, 114
onomatopoeia 74–75

parables 25
paralogisms 63
Parliament (band) 21
patriarchy 25, 43, 59, 60, 125
   see also Eurocentrism
Paul 22
phenomenological model 23–24
phenomenological reduction 47–48
phenomenology 17, 39–40, 43, 47–53, 79, 133
   and eidetic reduction 50–51
   and *epoche* 47–48, 49–50, 52
   and hermeneutics 54
   and noetic/noematic poles 49, 54, 57

and theology 52
and transcendental reduction 51–53
philosophy 18, 37, 48, 129
   linguistic 35
   metaphysics 44, 51, 52, 55, 118
   of religion 129–131, 133
   see also phenomenology
Pierce, Charles Sanders 12
Plato 10–11, 44
play/games 76, 77–78, 92
poetry 4, 21, 69, 92, 94
political aspects 6, 24–25, 27, 38–40, 63, 114
   and race 83, 108
   see also liberalism; neoliberalism
popup books 92, 95
predicates 13, 14, 15, 50, 57, 79–80, 90, 99
   and appropriation 121, 122
   and meaning 82–83
   and questions 31, 33, 80, 86, 104
prejudice 4, 6, 10, 17, 56–64, 71, 85, 107, 128
   Eurocentrism *see* Eurocentrism
   productive 57–59
premise-centered questioning 87
propaganda 63
propositionalist ideology 75–76
Proslogion (Anselm) 29
Prothero, Stephen 131–132
psychologism 40
psychology 28, 30, 37, 103
pure consciousness 48

queer theory 48, 127
questions 20, 30–36, 40–41, 67, 84–90, 129, 135
   and appropriation 120, 122
   behind-the-lines 103, 114
   between-the-lines 102, 105, 114
   beyond-the-lines 103–104, 105, 116
   and classic texts 110–111
   and embodiment 84–85
   four layers of 101–105, 107

genuine 35–36, 88, 127
and humanities 40
and interpretive communities
  112–113, 126–128
and meaning 33–34, 84, 85
on-the-lines 101–102, 105, 114
open-ended 34, 87
passivity of 31–32, 33
poles of 86–88
and predicates 31, 33, 80, 86
and prejudice 58–59
and reader's caprice 34–35
and reading 91, 101–105
and relationships 88–89
shared 32, 34, 113, 122, 127
and text 35–36, 96, 97–98
and topics 31
twelve kinds of 88
and understanding 31, 32, 32–33,
  72, 85, 87
and writer's intention 34
Quran 4, 42, 96, 128

racism 39, 44, 45, 54, 59, 62–63, 83, 108
  colorblind 62
rationality 3, 87
rationality-centered questioning 87
reader caprice 26, 29, 34–35
reading/readers 19, 20, 23–25, 30,
  91–92, 95–96
  aloud 95–96
  and classic texts *see* classic texts
  and critique of ideology 23, 24–25
  and dialogue 96, 97, 104
  and institutional model 23, 24
  and otherness 122
  and phenomenological model
    23–24
  and presumption of neutrality 62
  and questions 91, 101–105
  as social practice 123
  and "wax nose" problem 26
reasoning *see* logical fallacies
redemptive hegemony 125, 126
reference 14–15, 16

reflexivity 17, 43, 47, 51, 87, 112, 127
Reformation 43, 123
reification 13–14
relationality, two modes of 9–10
religion, as category 60
religious literacy 131–133
  and questioning 132–133
religious studies 52, 60–61, 129–134
  Christian bias of 129–130
  insularity of 130
  interdisciplinarity of 18, 130
  and Y structure 133–134
religious writing *see* sacred writings
Republic, The (Plato) 10–11
respectability politics 24–25, 83
responsibility 121, 126
rhetoric 42, 70, 127
  of signs 12
  of unspeakability 72
Ricoeur, Paul 14, 27, 54, 101, 114
  and discourse 71, 74
  and hermeneutical arc 117
  and predication 79, 80, 82
  and text 25, 28, 94–95, 98, 99, 122
  and traditions 109, 110
  and translation 65, 66
rights 45, 127
romantic hermeneutics 21–22, 109,
  113, 114
Rushd, Ibn 45, 122

sacred writings 2, 22–23, 24–25, 119
  see also Bible; Quran
Said, Edward 61, 63, 134
St. Clair, Raquel A. 25
salat, five pillars of 73
Sartre, Jean-Paul 46
Saussure, Ferdinand de 12
Schilbrack, Kevin 131, 132
Schleiermacher, Friedrich 21–22, 103,
  105, 118
science 19, 20, 21, 36, 37, 38–39, 40
  as god 38
  and religion 100–101
  and subjectivity 43

scientific method 21, 60
seesaw game 77–78
self 54–55, 56
self-consciousness *see* interpretive consciousness
semantic autonomy 25
semantics 13–15, 16, 17, 75
  and reference/sense 14–15
semiotics 11–13, 15, 75
sentences 1, 71, 72, 78–79, 83–84, 91–92, 114
  and complete thoughts 14–15, 16, 40, 89, 102
  and meaning/understanding 2, 8, 16, 33, 34, 40, 84, 85, 86, 89, 92
  and questions 16, 17, 18, 33, 34, 40, 70, 75, 78
  and signs 13, 14, 15, 79
  and texts 15
sentential meanings/subject 13–14, 15, 33, 49, 50, 86, 89–90
sexism 44, 59
Shariah law 73
Shirō, Matsumoto 55
Shoah 69, 70, 72
signifiers 12
signs 2, 3, 11–12, 13, 14, 15, 16, 74–76
  in Greek philosophy 74–75
Skloot, Rebecca 38
slavery 43, 45
Smith, Mitzi J. 24–25
social practices
  and discourse 72
  hegemonic 126
  and institutional power 124–125
  and interpretation 123–128
  and reading 123
social structures 53–54
sociology 37
Socrates 87, 89
sola scriptura 123, 124, 126
songs 2, 3, 10, 73, 92, 96, 116, 119
soul 55
speech 10, 13
stereotypes 44, 50–51

storytelling 45–46
subject 13–14, 15, 53, 57
  absence of 45–46
subjectivity 10, 43–46
  evolution of 43–44
  and interpretive consciousness 42, 45–47, 54
  and neoliberal capitalism 45
  and reading 96
  and sexism/racism 44–45
  of texts 26
  transcendent 60
  transcendental *see* transcendental subjectivity
suicide bombings 68, 70
synecdoche 23, 70
synthesis-centered questioning 88, 104

Taylor, Charles 3
telepathy 66–67
textbooks 7, 13, 60, 74, 94, 113
texting 9, 12
texts 2, 91–111
  and books, compared 1, 6–11, 28, 33, 91–96, 106, 112
  classic *see* classic texts
  and correctness of interpretation 19, 20, 25–26, 27, 28–29, 30
  and dialogue/listening 78, 96, 97–98, 100, 104, 107, 111, 115–116
  etymology of 8, 94
  and fitting questions 35–36
  and hermeneutical arc/circle/coil 117–119, 128, 133
  and institutional power 29, 106
  and questions 35–36, 96, 97–98
  and responsibility 121–122
  as semantic fields 93
  and speakers 95
  world of 99, 100, 102, 104, 112, 129
thesis-centered questioning 88
Thich Nhat Hanh 28

topics 31
traditions 87, 100–101, 107–110, 124, 130
transcendent subjectivity 60, 121
transcendental reduction 51–53
transcendental subjectivity 52–53, 54–55, 63–64
   and dialogue 64, 89
translation 65–66
Trump, Donald 38

understanding 11, 71–73, 77, 79, 91–92, 94–95, 134–135
   and questions 31, 32–33, 72, 85, 87
   restriction of 72–73
United States (US) 38, 39, 42, 63, 100, 131
9/11 attacks in (2001) 63
universals, eidetic 50, 51
universities 37
US Constitution 2, 42, 128

vaccines 38
validation 21
Vanhoozer, Kevin J. 92–93
Vayntrub, Jacqueline 127
video games 6

Warnke, Georgia 56, 58
"wax nose" problem 26
weaving 8, 94
Weiss, Gail 121
Welton, Donn 48, 51
white privilege/power 62, 63
white supremacy 6, 12, 38, 54, 59, 108, 126
Wikipedia 9
Wittgenstein, Ludwig 15, 68–69, 89, 90, 103, 115
Wolterstorff, Nicholas 22–23, 26, 28–29, 93, 106–107, 120–121
worldviews 61
writing therapy 89, 101
writing/writers 17–18, 19, 20–23, 30, 39, 42, 90
   and death of the author 26–27
   and dialogue with reader 97
   and empathy of reader 21
   and god 22–23
   and hermeneutic fallacies 28
   psychology of 103
   and shared questions 34
   transformational power of 97–101

Y structure 133–134
Yacub, Zera 45

www.ingramcontent.com/pod-product-compliance
Lightning Source LLC
Chambersburg PA
CBHW071847230426
43671CB00012B/2099